LEAD,
FOLLOW,
or
GET OUT OF
THE WAY

SECOND EDITION

*This book is dedicated to the legions of leaders, mentors,
and role models in all fields who have informed, instructed, and
inspired me over the years. Their leadership is a gift that keeps on giving.*

LEAD, FOLLOW, *or* GET OUT OF THE WAY

SECOND EDITION

How to Be a More Effective Leader in Today's Schools

ROBERT D. RAMSEY

CORWIN PRESS
A SAGE Publications Company
Thousand Oaks, California

For information:

Corwin Press
A Sage Publications Company
2455 Teller Road
Thousand Oaks, California 91320
www.corwinpress.com

Sage Publications Ltd.
1 Oliver's Yard
55 City Road
London EC1Y 1SP
United Kingdom

Sage Publications India Pvt. Ltd.
B-42, Panchsheel Enclave
Post Box 4109
New Delhi 110 017 India

Printed in the United States of America

Library of Congress Cataloging-in-Publication Data

Ramsey, Robert D.
Lead, follow, or get out of the way: How to be a more effective leader in today's schools/ Robert D. Ramsey—2nd ed.
   p. cm.
Includes bibliographical references and index.
ISBN 1-4129-1584-8 (cloth)—ISBN 1-4129-1585-6 (pbk.)
   1. Educational leadership—United States—Handbooks, manuals, etc. 2. School administrators—United States—Handbooks, manuals, etc. 3. School management and organization—United States—Handbooks, manuals, etc. I. Title.
LB2831.82.R36 2006
371.2'00973—dc22   2005008046

This book is printed on acid-free paper.

05   06   07   08   09   10   9   8   7   6   5   4   3   2   1

Acquisitions Editor:	Elizabeth Brenkus
Editorial Assistants:	Candice L. Ling, Jingle Vea
Production Editor:	Beth A. Bernstein
Typesetter:	C&M Digitals (P) Ltd.
Proofreader:	Dennis W. Webb
Indexer:	Molly Hall
Cover Designer:	Rose Storey

Contents

Preface to the Second Edition

Many of the precepts of school leadership spelled out in this guide transcend time limits. They worked yesterday, work today, and will work tomorrow. One of these enduring principles is that learning is a lynchpin of successful leadership.

Since the publication of the first edition of *Lead, Follow, or Get Out of the Way*, effective school leaders have learned some new skills and strategies and some new ways to apply old standards. That's why an updated edition is both timely and needed.

This new printing contains updated insights, fresh approaches to persistent challenges, and newly discovered responses to unprecedented developments.

If you are reading this manual for the first time, you will find a complete package of essential information and techniques to make you a more effective school leader today. If you are revisiting this book, you are in for an invigorating refresher course (School Leadership 101), complete with the latest tweaks and twists you need to maintain a competitive edge.

There are many managers in today's schools, but far fewer genuine leaders (God bless 'em). Reading or rereading this guide can help you move to the head of the class and stay there—if you let it.

But only you can choose whether you want to lead, follow, or get out of the way. Which will it be?

Preface to the First Edition

Graduate schools teach administrators about curriculum, budgets, discipline procedures, and school law; but who teaches them to be leaders? Nobody—until now!

Lead, Follow, or Get Out of the Way is a comprehensive leadership guide exclusively for school administrators. This unique handbook offers the prospective and practicing administrator alike practical lessons on how to think, act, plan, set priorities, manage time, and make decisions as an effective leader. It is an invaluable resource for principals, superintendents, and other administrators that pinpoints the specific know-how, skills, attitudes, and habits that separate effective leaders from run-of-the-mill school managers.

Unlike most professional handbooks, this unusual manual is designed to help any administrator move beyond performing routine management activities to functioning as a true leader. It covers every aspect of being a leader, from handling school politics, using leadership tools, and dealing with setbacks to managing change, getting the most out of people, and working smarter.

Each chapter is packed with school-tested advice and real-world examples of what readers need to know to become effective leaders in today's schools. Every section contains dozens of samples, figures, ready-to-use forms, and time-saving checklists to help apply the guide's practical lessons in leadership.

Lead, Follow, or Get Out of the Way is a far cry from the usual nuts-and-bolts (bits-and-pieces) manual on how to develop a certain kind of curriculum, build a master schedule, or handle specific day-to-day discipline problems. Instead, it is a practical and complete guide on how to change people, make things happen, and move any school organization forward as an effective leader.

More than ever before, the nation's schools cry out for leadership. Unfortunately, no one is systematically teaching today's administrators how to lead. School leaders are made, not born. But it doesn't happen unless someone helps them develop the necessary skills, techniques, and strategies that mark successful leaders. This handbook does just that.

If you're an aspiring principal or superintendent or a current administrator struggling with red tape, bureaucracy, regulation, and routine who wants to do more, this guide may be just what you've been waiting for—a user's manual for school leaders. It may be the best bet yet for releasing the real leader inside of you. There's nothing quite like it on the market today. Are you interested?

ACKNOWLEDGMENTS

No author is an island. Every published work is a collaboration and this one is no exception. That's why I want to acknowledge the vital assistance of Gracia Alkema, who saw the worth of and supported the work, and my wife, Joyce, whose magic transforms chicken scratches into a professionally prepared product. Without their help, the original publication would still be just another manuscript idea waiting to become a book.

In preparing this current revision, I am indebted to the many reviewers in the field who shared their insights, provided appropriate reality checks, and made helpful constructive criticisms. I also want to give special recognition to my patient editor, Elizabeth Brenkus, without whose prodding, support, encouragement, and cheerleading this edition would have remained in limbo.

Thanks to all of the above, this revision is not just a more up-to-date edition; it is a richer, more powerful resource for today's school leaders.

Corwin Press gratefully acknowledges the contributions of the following individuals:

C. Robert Maxfield
Superintendent
Farmington Public Schools
Farmington, MI

Jim Shaw
Clinical Professor
Department of Educational
    Administration
University of
    Wisconsin–Madison
Madison, WI

Howard W. Smith
Superintendent of Schools
Public Schools of the Tarrytowns
Tarrytown, NY

Gene M. Soloman
2003 NAESP National
    Distinguished Principal
Cavallini Middle School
Upper Saddle River, NJ

Mark J. White
Principal
Hintgen Elementary School
La Crosse, WI

About the Author

Robert D. Ramsey is a lifelong educator who has served as a "leader of leaders" in three award-winning school districts in two different states. His frontline experience includes positions as teacher, counselor, assistant principal, curriculum director, assistant superintendent, acting superintendent, and adjunct professor.

Most recently, he has served as associate superintendent in the St. Louis Park (MN) schools, where every school has been designated by the federal government as a National School of Excellence. Ramsey is now working full time as a freelance writer in Minneapolis.

Throughout his distinguished career, Ramsey's writings, including *Secondary School Principal's Survival Guide, Administrator's Comprehensive School Discipline Guide, The Principal's Book of Lists*, and *501 Tips for Teachers*, have helped countless teachers and administrators improve their work and lives and reach their full potential. In *Lead, Follow, or Get Out of the Way*, this same practical assistance is available to help administrators at all levels become the effective leaders they want to be and can be—and that our children need them to be!

Introduction

WHERE HAVE ALL THE GOOD LEADERS GONE?

If your school system is looking for a new elementary or secondary principal, a superintendent, or some other key administrator, good luck! The pickin's are slim.

Not so many years ago, job postings for school administrators attracted literally hundreds of applications from highly qualified candidates. Today, the flood of applications for school administrative openings has diminished to a trickle. Worse yet, the applicants who are available and interested aren't always high-quality leadership material.

It shouldn't be a great surprise that fewer and fewer outstanding men and women want to become principals and superintendents today. Unfortunately, there are plenty of good reasons for this lack of interest. Where have all the good leaders gone?

Higher salaries and potential lifelong earnings in business and industry have traditionally siphoned off a lot of leadership talent from the public schools. There have always been a certain number of outstanding teachers with the potential for becoming outstanding school leaders who grow tired of struggling on low pay and leave the profession for higher stakes in the private sector.

Historically, however, there have also always been enough dedicated educators who have stuck it out to become dynamic, effective school administrators. Within recent memory, most sizable school districts consistently had a pool of talented teachers trained and ready to step into administrative leadership positions. This isn't true today. Why?

The answer is simple. Sometimes, it's not much fun being a school administrator. The pay isn't commensurate with the challenges. The hours are long. The perks are limited. Respect for public school officials is waning. The money to support quality schools is hard to come by. The tenure is tentative. (The average stay for urban superintendents in America today is less than 4 years.) Worst of all, the problems facing today's school leaders are enormous and often seem almost unsolvable. Who needs it?

A sampling of the almost limitless problems confronting contemporary school leaders includes the following:

- School violence
- Poverty
- Cheating
- Escalating costs
- Physical and sexual abuse
- Teen pregnancy
- Mixed messages
- Petty politics
- Missing children
- Student depression
- Textbook controversies
- Throwaway kids
- Underfunding
- Dropouts
- Racism
- Sexism
- Social promotions
- Grade inflation
- Militant labor unions
- Labor disputes
- Runaway dads
- Taxpayers' revolts
- Student smoking
- Student truancy
- Politicization of education
- Staff absenteeism
- Epidemic eating disorders
- Homeless pupils and families
- Regulation and red tape
- Growing popularity of homeschooling
- Guns, gangs, and gore on the school grounds
- Drugs (repeated studies show that it is equally easy to get guns and drugs in many schools)
- School bashing by politicians and the media
- Gambling addiction among teens (which is now spreading even faster than new casinos are being opened)
- Untenable tenure laws that make it virtually impossible to get rid of incompetent teachers
- School prayer debates
- Failing bond issues and defeated levy referendums
- Lack of a clear and consistent mission
- Too many interest groups, too many constituencies, and too many bosses

- School shootings
- Sexually transmitted diseases (STDs)
- Teen suicide
- Out-of-control litigation
- Competition from private schools
- Dysfunctional families (administrators commonly complain about families falling apart all around them)
- Crime (did you hear about the principal who starts off each day patrolling the parking lot looking for pimps?)
- Media misrepresentation of facts
- Deteriorating discipline and a growing epidemic of disrespect
- Controversies over teaching creationism versus evolution
- Polarized school boards (unfortunately, the scarcity of educational leadership extends all the way to elected boards of education)

The list goes on and on. The proliferation of problems confronting school administrators is mind-boggling. It might even be funny, if it weren't so pathetic—and so important.

Schools today have all of their own problems to solve and all of society's problems as well. Somewhere along the way, Americans decided that the public schools should fix everything for everybody. Unfortunately, the schools can't say "no."

Now the schools themselves need fixing, and there aren't enough trained fixers to do the job. The biggest problem facing today's schools is a shortage of leaders who are trained and capable of solving all of the schools' other problems.

It doesn't have to be that way. It's time to reinvent (and in some cases, resurrect) leadership in the nation's schools. We need to recruit and train new, prospective leaders. Just as importantly, we need to retrain current administrators to become true leaders, not merely caretaker managers.

There are more than enough good administrators still in today's schools who want to be effective leaders capable of solving the myriad problems outlined above. Someone just has to teach them how to lead.

CAN EVERYDAY ADMINISTRATORS LEARN "LEADERSHIP"? YOU BET!

Effective school leaders (like most leaders in other fields) are made, not born. It doesn't happen, however, unless someone teaches them the know-how, skills, habits, attitudes, and strategies that separate true leaders from run-of-the-mill managers.

Unfortunately, too many current administrators feel bogged down in bureaucracy, bound by red tape, and overwhelmed with "administrivia." They don't have time to be leaders. They're too busy dancing from one hot coal to another. They've never been given the tools or time to become leaders. They need help in learning how to move beyond performing perfunctory management functions to the next level of service—leadership.

Up to now, administrators have had to learn how to be leaders by trial and error, initiation under fire, and on-the-job experience, with the help of an occasional mentor or support network along the way. That's the hard way. An easier way is to tap into the rich and growing body of professional literature on school leadership. This concise sourcebook is a good place to start.

Being a school leader can become exciting and rewarding again, once people are adequately trained and equipped to tackle today's challenges. It's fun when you know how to solve problems.

Ironically, education is the answer to education's biggest problem. Only this time, what is needed is education for practicing and prospective school leaders on how to think, make decisions, solve problems, plan for the future, communicate successfully, allocate time efficiently, manage politics, and get the most out of other people and themselves as effective leaders.

Such training is beginning to happen in pockets of graduate schools around the country and in certain special leadership training programs, such as the Bush Fellowship Program at the University of Minnesota and the Center for Creative Leadership in Greensboro, North Carolina. This book can help as well. Training effective school leaders starts by recognizing the unique aspects of leadership in the very public arena of the public schools.

HOW LEADERSHIP IN SCHOOLS IS DIFFERENT

Leadership skills are largely transferable. What works for management usually works for union leaders, too. What works in the corporate boardroom works in the school board boardroom as well. Nevertheless, there are both substantive and subtle differences between leadership in the public and private sectors. That's why leadership in schools requires certain special abilities and approaches.

School superintendents, principals, and other administrators differ from most leaders in other fields in several significant ways:

- School leaders head up organizations with no clear and consistent mission (Americans can't agree on what they want their schools to do or be).
- School leaders contend with chronic uncertainty about funding and often have little or no control over their sources of funding.
- School leaders don't always know who their customers are (students? parents? taxpayers?).
- School leaders have no quality control over their raw materials (students). They have to take whatever the parents send them.
- School leaders have to make daily decisions in the midst of all the constituencies involved. They function in a fishbowl. Many work

under stringent "open meeting laws." Being a school leader means operating in a constant crossfire without the luxury of being able to distance yourself in order to make a more objective decision.

- School leaders exercise a wider span of control, play to more diverse audiences, and serve a broader range of constituencies than do most leaders in the private sector (see Exhibit I.1).
- School leaders work for results that are not always readily measurable. For school leaders, the payoff is often years away.
- The decisions made by school leaders affect more segments of the community than do the decisions of leaders in most other fields.
- School leaders work in a highly politicized environment and report to a politically elected board of directors. What CEO in the private sector would stand for that?
- School leaders have to be accountable to more "bosses" than most leaders in the private sector.
- School leaders are expected to perform both leadership and management functions, unlike leaders in many other fields.
- School leaders work in a field where everyone considers themselves experts.

Leadership is always difficult. Leadership in schools is even a little more tricky and complex than in most private sector situations. In schools, as in most factories, shops, and offices, being a manager is challenging enough; but being a true leader is a lot tougher.

THE DIFFERENCE BETWEEN EFFECTIVE SCHOOL LEADERS AND RUN-OF-THE-MILL MANAGERS

Most school administrators today, including many superintendents, are stuck. They're limited to functioning strictly as managers.

Managers deal with the moment. Managers make do, monitor, and maintain. They manage what is there without doing much to make it better. Being a manager is hard work and not much fun.

Leaders, on the other hand, energize and excite the organization and the people in it by showing what it can become. Leaders deal with visions, dreams, and possibilities. They shape the organization, involve others in creating its future, and model ways to make it happen. Being a leader is harder than being a manager; but it's a lot more fun. See Table I.1 for a list of the differences between leaders and managers.

Most administrators aren't stuck being managers by choice. It's not all their fault. Bureaucracy, red tape, paperwork, legal precautions, and overregulation favor managing and are no friends of leadership. Most managers want to do more and be more.

Exhibit I.1   School Leaders Play to Many Audiences

Students	Federal government
Parents	General public
Staff	Media
School board	Professional organizations
City officials	Universities and colleges
Taxpayers	County officials
District administrators	Athletic conferences
Family	Businesses
Friends	Health department
Feeder schools	Contractors
Service clubs	Chamber of Commerce
Alumni	Fire marshals
State boards	Code inspectors
Accrediting agencies	Realtors
Labor unions	Police
Athletic boosters	Neighbors of the school
Legislatures	PTA
Social agencies	

Most average school administrators would like to become true leaders but don't have the time and don't know how to make the time. They don't know how to create a shared vision. They don't know how to empower and get the most out of people. No one ever taught them the decision-making, problem-solving, political, and communication skills and the know-how necessary to move an organization forward. They don't know how to get beyond caretaking. They simply don't know how to lead.

But all of this can be changed through real-world leadership training. Leadership is learnable. Good managers can be transformed into success-ful leaders. Reading this guide is a good way to start. The first lesson is to understand what marks an effective school leader for the 21st century.

WHAT IT TAKES TO BE AN EFFECTIVE SCHOOL LEADER TODAY

To successfully manage today's schools takes what it has always taken: hard work; dedication; some knowledge of subject matter, learning theory,

Table I.1   The Differences Between Leaders and Managers

Managers	Leaders
React to the crisis du jour	Proact, anticipate problems
Put out fires, practice damage control	Practice crisis prevention
Accept existing roles and implement established objectives	Create dreams, identify and clarify the mission of the organization
Attend to details (the day-to-day routines of running the school or system)	Attend to intangibles (values, ideas, etc.)
Conform, cope with the system	Push the envelope, change the system
Focus on the here and now	Focus on (create) the future
Allocate existing resources	Create or find new resources
Work with bits and pieces	Work with the whole
"Boss" people, give orders	Empower people, give choices
Nurture control	Instruct and inspire, nurture the culture of the organization
Carry out policies and directions, follow the prescribed path	Find new ways, define new places to go
Deal with problems	Deal with possibilities
Make rules	Set goals
Meet expectations	Set new standards
Criticize	Cheerlead
Never have enough time	Make time

and child development; and basic people skills. To successfully lead today's schools, however, requires even more.

Exhibit I.2 lists the qualities that distinguish effective leaders from run-of-the-mill managers. No leader possesses all of these traits, but all leaders possess most of them. Each trait can be learned, acquired, or developed. If you want to become an effective school leader, these qualities are what you should work on.

Of these characteristics, the first and last are the most compelling and important. The biggest differences between effective leaders and also-rans, wannabes, and run-of-the-mill managers are authenticity and passion. ("Timeless leadership is always about character, and it is always about authenticity."—Warren Bennis, business author). All significant leaders are true to themselves (authenticity) and care deeply about what they do (passion). We've all known administrators new to positions of authority who adopt a false persona because they think it makes them more leader-like. They're wrong. Staff, parents, and community members are quick to spot phonies. Kids do it best of all. And no one knowingly follows a phony. Why would they? Would you?

My dictionary defines *authentic* as genuine and worthy of trust, reliance, and belief. As it turns out, that could also be the definition of an effective school leader.

The truth is that there is no single leadership style or personality type. That's why the best advice for any practicing or prospective leader is simply: Be yourself—be true to the best instincts inside you. Anything less betrays your core values and holds out a false promise to the people who are supposed to follow you.

With authentic leaders, what you see is what you get. They are open, honest, and true to their word. They say what they mean and they keep their commitments. They lead with a sense of purpose and value principles over ego. Authentic leaders naturally opt for doing the right thing, not just for the easiest, most convenient, most popular, or most self-serving course of action. They live their values every day, on and off the job.

Bill George, former CEO of the nationally recognized, value-driven Medtronics corporation, identifies five basic components of authentic leadership:

1. Purpose (in schools, we often call it our mission)

2. Values (a consistent set of beliefs)

3. Heart (this is where passion enters in)

4. Relationships (connectedness with others around a common purpose)

5. Self-discipline (the discipline to do what's right)

To run the daily affairs of the school, you may not have to possess all the attributes of authenticity or be driven by a passion for your work. But you can't rise above the ordinary without these traits. If you are unwilling to lay your true self on the line or if being a school administrator is a passionless job to you, you can never be more than a manager.

Authenticity and passion may be inborn. But the remainder of the qualities of an effective leader can be taught, nurtured, and sharpened. The following chapters will show you how.

Exhibit I.2   Qualities of an Effective 21st-Century School Leader

1. Authenticity (phonies don't make good leaders)
2. Tenacity and persistence (good leaders never give up on students or themselves)
3. Ambiguity tolerance (the capacity to live with partial fulfillment and unsolved problems)
4. Flexibility
5. A commitment to excellence
6. Self-confidence
7. A reality-based attitude
8. Self-discipline
9. Technological know-how
10. Commitment to lifelong learning
11. Optimism and hope (a positive view of life, students, and the future)
12. A philosophy of risk taking (the willingness to be uncomfortable)
13. Planning, organizing, and prioritizing skills (the ability to be more organized than you appear to be)
14. Fascination and comfort with change
15. Buoyancy (ability to bounce back from setbacks)
16. Goal-setting skills
17. Decision-making and problem-solving skills
18. Time management skills
19. Political savvy
20. Higher-level thinking skills
21. Communication skills (reading, writing, speaking, and listening)
22. A professional image
23. The ability to get the most out of people
24. The ability to close the deal (finish projects, get things done)
25. A commitment to ethical (principled) leadership
26. Common sense and uncommon sensitivity
27. The willingness to be intuitive (trust your instincts)
28. Good physical and mental health and a balanced life
29. Genuine love and concern for kids
30. Passion

1

Making Decisions

People expect their leaders to make decisions. That's what leadership is all about. Schools are no different. All school personnel respect a decisive leader (at least as long as the leader's decisions work out and are popular and painless). Firm decision making and strong leadership are synonymous in the mind of school employees and patrons.

Conversely, principals, superintendents, and other school administrators who have difficulty in making decisions are judged to be weak and ineffectual. No one respects a wishy-washy, vacillating leader. In fact, the most damning criticism of school leaders is that "they can't make up their minds."

The trouble is that making decisions isn't easy in today's rapidly changing school environments. There are too many confusing data. There are too many conflicting opinions. There are too many choices. There is too much gray and not enough black and white. There are few sure things.

To make matters even worse, wrong decisions can cost money, reputations, and even jobs. It's no wonder that many would-be leaders hedge, stonewall, and back away from decision making.

No one ever said it was easy to make decisions as a school leader. If it were, there would be lots more leaders and fewer followers. Of course, everyone has to make decisions in his or her everyday life. When you are a school leader, the difference is that your decisions affect many other people's lives, and everyone is watching while you make them (some hoping you will blow it). Nevertheless, if you want to be a leader, and not just a caretaker administrator, you have to make tough choices, solve real problems, make good decisions, and make those decisions in a timely manner.

Fortunately, there are some insider tips that can help any school leader make better, quicker, and easier decisions. This process starts by deciding what to decide.

WHOSE DECISION IS IT?

Not all decisions properly belong to the leader. There's no rule that says everything has to be resolved at the top. If the leader has to make all the major decisions, there are too many useless lieutenants in the organization. No department, school, or school system can afford to wait around for the leader to decide every important issue.

The first step in effective decision making is to sort out whose decision it is to make. The person in charge doesn't have a monopoly on wisdom and certainly doesn't have time to make every minute decision. Why waste your time and your reputation over decisions you shouldn't be making in the first place? Any decision is more likely to be the right decision if the right person has made it. The trick is to know which decisions to make and which ones to delegate.

Whenever any leader makes decisions that should be made by someone else, time is wasted, inefficiencies occur, feelings are hurt, resentments crop up, the decisions are less enthusiastically received, and the results are often less than satisfactory. Some decisions just logically belong to other staff members.

Curriculum decisions should largely be made in the curriculum department and in the classroom. Most business decisions should be made in the business office. Some decisions should rightfully rest with the school board. A good leader learns when to pass the buck and when "the buck stops here."

The best way to determine and assign responsibility for decision making is to ask and answer these questions:

1. Who is closest to the problem or situation? (The best decisions are usually made closest to home.)

2. Who has the greatest expertise (i.e., background, skills, information, and know-how) to make the decision?

3. Who has time to gather the information and to weigh the consequences in order to make this decision?

4. Who can most easily make the decision in the shortest amount of time?

5. Who has the resources to implement the decision?

6. Who is most politically influential in this matter?

7. Who will ultimately be held accountable for the decision?

Unless the leader's name comes up as the answer to most of the questions, there's good reason to consider letting (or appointing) someone else to do the deciding. Of course, it's always important to make it absolutely clear exactly who is expected to decide each issue.

In baseball, fielders sometimes let a ball drop because no one is sure who is supposed to catch it. Administrative teams can drop the ball too if signals are unclear. Whenever you delegate a decision, be sure the responsible party knows about it.

School personnel appreciate leaders who make decisions; but they appreciate even more leaders who empower others to make their own decisions within their appropriate areas of expertise and/or responsibility.

Naturally, there are some decisions that can't be sidestepped and clearly must be made by the leader in charge. These include the following:

- Decisions that are the most important and far-reaching for the leader's area of authority
- Decisions that are part of the job (in the job description)
- Decisions that only the leader can carry out
- Decisions that only the leader has the special information or expertise to make
- Decisions that everyone in the organization expects the leader to make

In addition to these guidelines, the following "rules" have helped many successful leaders determine which decisions to make, which decisions to leave for others, and which ones to avoid making altogether:

1. Never make a decision about matters you don't understand without getting help.

2. Never make a decision when you are angry.

3. Never make a decision just to show off.

4. Never make a decision that is illegal, violates your professional code of ethics (see Chapter 12), or is not in the best interests of the children.

5. Never make a decision for which others will get all the credit (or the blame).

6. Never make a decision just to punish or keep someone else from making it.

7. Never make a decision that feels wrong.

Using all of these guideposts can make it easier for administrators to decide what to decide. When the decision is clearly the leader's to make, it should be made on the basis of the best information and the best ideas available.

WHERE DO GOOD IDEAS COME FROM?

Decisions shouldn't be made in a vacuum. Every leader needs a constant flow of new ideas in order to make decisions that are sound, timely, and relevant. Without a continuing supply of fresh ideas for solving problems and making decisions, no leader or school organization can maintain an edge.

The good news is that school leaders don't have to come up with all of the answers, solutions, and bright ideas by themselves. They do, however, need to be able to recognize good ideas when they see them and to access them when needed.

Knowing where to look for answers and new insights is the easy part. Good ideas can come from anywhere. Anyone in the organization, including students, can have a good idea sometimes, whereas no one (including the leader) has good ideas all the time.

Fortunately, good ideas are a plentiful and replenishable resource. The best administrators constantly keep their antennae tuned to pick up worthwhile ideas for improved decision making wherever they find them.

Part of being a successful leader is knowing how to (a) promote innovative thinking, (b) tap into staff and student creativity, (c) sort out those ideas that really work from those that merely sound good, and (d) incorporate good ideas into the decision-making process quickly and easily. This starts by developing a school culture that values employees' input and suggestions and makes it easy for staff members and students to be heard (see the form below).

The role of an effective leader is to create a climate that welcomes, supports, and rewards innovative thinking and problem solving. When this happens, any school can become an "idea factory" that consistently produces the creative thinking necessary to drive sound decision making.

If you want students, administrators, teachers, and other staff members to routinely come up with workable suggestions, solutions, answers, improvements, and new approaches, you have to trust them. Everyone in the organization should have permission to take risks. It has to be OK to fail, have a bad idea, or hold a minority opinion occasionally. The best administrators know that sometimes it even pays to celebrate mistakes and flawed decisions, as well as successes.

Other characteristics of a solution-oriented environment include the following:

- A "we-can" attitude has been established. There is an unspoken agreement that no problem is impossible to solve—difficult maybe; but not impossible.
- There is an open climate in which people at all levels really listen to each other.
- Solutions are not limited by turf boundaries.
- Individuals who have good ideas get credit for them. Leaders share both credit and blame.

Feedback Form

Good ideas can come from anywhere. Please use this form to share your ideas, suggestions, and solutions. Use the back of the form for any diagrams, sketches, or schematics that may help to explain your idea.

1. Statement of issue or problem:

2. Here's what I think we should do:

3. Why we should do it:

4. What it will take to do it (time, resources, etc.):

5. The biggest difficulty with my idea and how to overcome it:

6. What I will do personally to make my idea work:

- Tough problem are assigned to those who know the most about the issues involved, not just to someone who has an official title.
- "Devil's advocates" are built into the organization. Most intelligence agencies feature a subunit ("Red Team") whose members' job it is to act as contrarians and question all conclusions. All organizations, including schools, should have their own Red Team.
- Staff members, at all levels, have time to think.
- Problems are viewed as everyone's business.
- Information is shared freely throughout the organization. No one (not even the leader—especially not the leader) hoards or rations out information.
- The culture encourages questions. (There are no dumb questions, only dumb answers.)
- No idea is crushed before it has a chance to fly.
- Decisions and actions are based on reality. People pay more attention to hard data than to wishful thinking.
- Brainstorming is a way of life, not an occasional event.
- Identifying and acknowledging problems is "in," while denial and finger pointing are "out."
- The staff includes a mix of left and right brainers.
- Teamwork is the norm.
- Work is fun.

When the leader applies an attitude of acceptance and promotes the solution-oriented characteristics above, the generation of new ideas for decision making can become a habit in any school setting.

It also pays to remember that some of the best solutions, ideas, and answers are stumbled across by chance or accident. Serendipity can be a form of inspiration. The germs of good ideas can be found anywhere. Sound decision making is often just a matter of paying attention.

When everyone in the organization is constantly challenged to look for and think about solutions and fresh approaches, there's never a shortage of creative ideas to assist in decision making. One good idea follows another in a continuous stream. Creativity becomes routine, and decision making becomes a whole lot easier.

Some schools consistently come up with the best solutions and decisions. Others always seem to make poor choices and bad decisions. What makes the difference? Often, it's a leader who knows how to solicit and sort through diverse input from a variety of sources.

INPUT: HOW TO GET IT, WHERE TO GET IT, AND WHEN TO IGNORE IT

Most decisions are only as good as the input upon which they are based. Getting valid and varied input, and making the most of it, are important parts of the decision-making process.

Effective leaders don't make decisions in isolation. When possible, they rely on input from others to help them determine appropriate courses of action. At the same time, there are limits to the use of such feedback. Just as not all decisions can or should be made by a leader acting alone, neither should all decisions be made entirely by plebiscites. The best leaders know when to get reliable input, how to get it, and how to use it.

Input is only valuable when those giving it feel comfortable with their leaders and feel free to express opinions honestly. The conditions conducive to obtaining open and honest input don't happen by accident. "Idea factories" are created by design, not by chance. Below are five additional ways to foster a climate that generates helpful input and guards against dishonest feedback at the same time:

1. Hire people who don't all think alike. (If all staff members always agree, some are useless.) To facilitate creative problem solving and enhance decision making, it often pays to have both left- and right-brain thinkers on the payroll.

2. Make it easy to get feedback, ideas, suggestions, and reactions to the top. Be accessible. Eliminate paper and procedural obstacles. Try reserving an e-mail address or hotline number exclusively for staff suggestions and ideas.

3. Hold brainstorming sessions when needed. (Be careful, however, to keep such sessions from deteriorating into "blame-storming" sessions. What are needed are answers, not excuses.) Involve everyone who has a stake in the final decision or outcome—including students.

4. Urge teachers and other staff members to bring back at least one "crazy idea" (solution) from every conference or seminar they attend.

5. Routinely challenge staff members by asking "What if?" and "Why don't we?" questions.

When effective school leaders need input to help in making an important decision, what they ask and how they ask depends largely on the nature and timing of the decision at hand.

The potential sources of input are usually plentiful and easily accessible. In most school settings, input can readily be solicited from subordinates, peers, coworkers, superiors, mentors, unions, professional organizations, and a variety of other personal and professional networks, as well as from individual students and student organizations. Through the Internet, it is now even possible to gather input worldwide. No school leader has to suffer from a shortage of advisors. The challenge is to pick the right sources and ask the right questions.

The more far-reaching a decision is, the more widespread the sources of input should be. A rule of thumb for many successful leaders is to seek input primarily from those who have some specific knowledge about the issue in question and who care enough about it to give it some thoughtful consideration. It's not always a good idea, however, to ask for advice from those who may benefit directly from or have a vital selfish interest in the final decision. It pays to consider the source of input. Only a very naïve (and usually short-lived) leader accepts all input at face value.

There are lots of ways to gather input for decision making. Which method is the most useful and practical depends on the significance, scope, and complexity of the decision and the timing involved. Methods of obtaining feedback range from very informal approaches to highly sophisticated opinion-gathering techniques. Some of the most widely used strategies include the following:

- Just listening to casual conversations (eavesdropping with a purpose) to pick up hints about existing attitudes and sentiments regarding the question under consideration (It pays to note what people aren't saying, as well as what they are saying.)
- Meeting with individuals and small groups to discuss the pros and cons of the issue
- Setting aside time to be available for anyone who cares enough or feels strongly enough to show up and share his or her views
- Employing formal focus groups to sample opinions or reactions
- Asking to receive advice by e-mail and/or voice mail
- Looking at what the school's suggestion box has to offer (Caution: Be wary of unsigned advice. On important issues, accountability is more important than anonymity.)
- Letting others (e.g., administrative assistants, secretaries, department heads) be your eyes and ears and report on the "buzz" within the organization
- Taking a survey or poll (It can be as simple as asking for a show of hands.)
- Requiring stakeholders to make forced choices between alternatives, to rank options or to rate ideas and proposals on a scale of 1–10
- Being open to receiving petitions from constituents
- Taking a nonbinding straw vote (Or putting the issue to a formal vote, which is never a wise move unless the leader is willing to be bound by the outcome.)

For most school leaders, gathering input or feedback is the easy part. The difficult part is sorting it out, interpreting it, and figuring out how to use it (if at all). There are times when it doesn't pay to seek input from any source.

Effective leaders refrain from soliciting input when

- There is insufficient time to get adequate feedback.
- The right decision is obvious and clear-cut.

- Others do not have enough background or information to provide meaningful input.
- There may be a conflict of interest for the potential sources of input.
- There's a strong likelihood that others will provide only the kind of input they think the leader wants to hear (good answers instead of real ones).
- The nature of the decision is such that it must be based solely on the leader's judgment.

There are also times when wise leaders largely ignore any input they've received from others and choose to decide the matter strictly on their own. These include situations where

- The input received is confusing, or there are too many conflicting opinions from which to discern any definitive direction.
- The leader knows something others do not or cannot know.
- The leader feels strongly that the direction indicated by the input received is wrong and is willing to accept responsibility for making a different decision.

When making a decision without the benefit of input from others, it sometimes helps to outline or write down alternative solutions, including the risks and ramifications involved. It can be as easy as preparing a simple "balance sheet" (see the template below) or doing some "decision mapping" by creating a paper trail tracing the possible outcomes of various courses of action under consideration.

When advice from others is sought, it's important to remember that input is only one factor in decision making. Gathering feedback is just a single step in the process. Sometimes, seeking input is merely an excuse to put off making a final decision.

DATA-DRIVEN DECISION MAKING: AN OLD TOOL WITH NEW IMPORTANCE

Of course, input comes in many forms. Not all of it emanates from advisors, observers, or stakeholders. For school leaders, more and more decisions are based on the objective input of hard data—particularly test scores. Leaders in all fields have always engaged in data-driven decision making; but today's school officials are required to do it by law (e.g., No Child Left Behind legislation).

More than ever before, administrators are functioning in an age of accountability based on results-oriented standards and measured by test performance. Increasingly, all school leaders are responsible not just for what is done to and with students but for specific measurable outcomes.

Decision-Making Balance Sheet

Suggested course of action:

Pros	Cons
Short Term	Short Term
1.	1.
2.	2.
3.	3.
4.	4.
5.	5.
Long Term	Long Term
1.	1.
2.	2
3.	3
4.	4
5.	5.

Weighting Factors

• Important

•• Somewhat important

••• Very important

Since the federal government, most state legislatures, and many local school districts have undertaken some form of Comprehensive School Reform (CSR), principals and superintendents are under enormous pressure to meet or exceed external standards, using test scores as evidence. The pressure to document achievement is so intense that some wags have suggested passage of new legislation—the "No Principal Left Behind" law. Obviously, data-driven decision making related to student achievement is a critical feature of the contemporary educational landscape.

The truth, however, is that basing decisions on hard data is nothing new for most school leaders. Good administrators and teachers have always used assessment results to drive differentiated instruction (diagnostic and prescriptive teaching) and linked professional development to improving results. What's new is a movement to base administrative and instructional decisions almost exclusively on test scores.

Data-driven decision making is a valuable strategy for all leaders—especially school leaders. But it's not enough. The challenge for today's principals and superintendents is to use test results and other objective data as only one decision-making tool among many.

There is more to be learned than what is codified in government-adopted standards or measured by mandated tests. Effective leaders make the decisions required by the data, the new standards, and the current system of accountability. But they don't stop there. Students are more than test scores. And there are valid sources of input that reach beyond available objective data, and decisions to make based on the information provided by these other sources.

Dealing with heightened accountability and relentless results-oriented scrutiny is a new kind of decision making for some administrators. Fortunately, the following guidelines can help any school leader make the most effective use of data-driven decision making:

- Respect the limitations of test scores or other objective data. Any set of data is merely a snapshot in time, while real learning is a moving picture. Try to base major decisions on patterns and trends, rather than on isolated results.
- Be sure you understand what the data are telling you. Initial evidence can be misleading and premature conclusions mistaken. For example, overall scores may be high, but a closer look may reveal significant achievement gaps between subgroups of students. Likewise, a low school ranking on test scores may not mean poor teaching, but may merely signify that a few too many students were absent on test day. Always break down data and look beneath the surface before making any firm decisions.
- Always gather a variety of data—not just the data required by government mandates. Some decisions require observation and anecdotal data, as well as test scores.

- Don't base decisions just on negative data (low scores). Make choices based on evidence of strengths as well.
- Take action to reduce the pressure, paranoia, and tension associated with tests required to meet graduation standards. Schedule some stress relievers and strictly-for-fun activities during testing periods. You'll get better data and make better decisions as a result.
- Use hard data to decide how to help all individuals and groups of students to improve, not just to choose who to penalize and how much.

Basing decisions on objective data is here to stay. But as with most aspects of decision making, patience can often be a virtue and a leader's best friend.

PROCRASTINATION IS A DECISION—SOMETIMES, THE RIGHT ONE

Effective leaders understand that deciding not to decide is a decision in itself. Procrastination is often a sign of laziness, inefficiency, incompetence, or cowardice. Sometimes, however, procrastination can be a conscious tactical strategy employed by a shrewd decision maker.

There are conditions under which putting off making a decision is the right decision. Procrastination can be a valuable tool if you know how and when to use it.

The following are examples of occasions in which procrastination may be the right decision:

- Not all the important or relevant data are yet available.
- No good solution is immediately apparent, but things may get better with time so that, eventually, no decision will have to be made after all.
- More time to think or search for alternatives may prove helpful.
- Focusing on the decision at hand is distracting attention from more sensitive or controversial ones (using procrastination as a smokescreen).
- Reinforcements are on the way, such as new money, new personnel, or new legislation.
- Allowing an "incubation" period may result in a better decision. (Sometimes, letting the subconscious mind work on a problem for a while yields a more creative solution.)
- Keeping people guessing about the outcome is stimulating interest and keeping everyone on their toes. (Anticipation can be energizing. When this happens, leaders may want to capitalize on the situation for a time.)

- There's a strong likelihood that pressure may dissipate and interested parties may lose interest over time, making the final decision easier to determine and implement.
- It's a lose-lose situation, and the leader wants to postpone the inevitable for as long as possible. ("Put off the evil time as long as you can."—Proverb).

Whenever a school leader determines that procrastination is the best decision for the moment, there are lots of ways to carry it out. The tools of procrastination are many and varied:

- Forming a committee or task force to study the issue (School personnel are notorious for this. If it's a particularly knotty problem, you can call it a "Blue Ribbon" Task Force. They take longer to deliberate.)
- Asking for more information, data, or input
- Conducting extensive background research
- Taking the matter "under advisement"
- Claiming that other issues have priority and must take precedent
- Seeking legal counsel
- Hiring a consultant
- Waiting for the legislature (or congress or the school board) to convene or adjourn
- Conducting lengthy surveys or opinion polls
- "Foot dragging"—performing every step of the decision-making process at a snail's pace

There are so many strategies for delaying decision making that procrastination can become an art form. Even when procrastination is the right thing to do, eventually a "real" decision will have to be made. At that point, the process is no secret.

REAL-WORLD STEPS IN DECISION MAKING

When it's time to "bite the bullet," there's no magic to decision making. Everyone follows essentially the same process. Effective leaders just do it better, quicker, and easier than most. Anyone, however, can improve with practice.

The "10 Classic Steps in Decision Making" are the following:

1. Acknowledge that a decision needs to be made, and identify the issues. (Take ownership of the problem.)

2. Define the limits of the issue or problem. (Gather data. Frame the questions.)

3. Clarify the issues involved. (Sort out cause and effect. Name the parts of the problem.)

4. Search for solutions. (Try listing alternative remedies or courses of action. Develop a pool of possibilities.)

5. Narrow the list. (Screen the alternatives.)

6. Test the possibilities. (Send up trial balloons. Bounce ideas off others.)

7. Select the preferred solution.

8. Take action. (Try the solution.)

9. Evaluate the results.

10. Maintain the solution if it works. (Modify and adjust it if needed.) If the chosen remedy doesn't work, repeat the process.

The shorthand version of this decision-making process is simply

What's wrong?	What are our choices?	Which one is best?	Let's do it!

See the decision-making process graphic below for a detailed example of the process. The same steps apply to all decisions, great or small. The importance of the decision commonly determines how long it takes to work through the process. Making a snap decision, however, is almost always a mistake.

If time is short, effective leaders may speed up the steps; but they seldom skip or eliminate any. When stuck, it often pays to revisit the steps or to start over.

Even though all decision makers follow the same steps, the best share certain traits that enable them to use the process to their greatest advantage. Many people possess these same characteristics but often don't exercise or develop them to their full potential. The qualities that mark successful decision makers are the following:

- A capacity for clear thinking
- Open-mindedness
- The ability to make up their minds relatively quickly
- A good memory (for previous decisions, what has worked, and what has failed)
- A willingness to try new and varied approaches
- The ability to absorb many points of view
- A realistic understanding of "what's going on out there"

An Example of the Decision-Making Process

(1) Receive reports of violence on school grounds (Identify the problem and gather data.)	(2) Talk to victims, witnesses, teachers, student leaders, gang members, etc.	(3) Determine causes: Racism? Bullying? Gang turf battles? (Sort issues.)
(4) Identify solutions: Stiffer penalties? More security? Conflict resolution training? (List remedies.)	(5) What will the budget allow? What will the community support? (Narrow choices.)	(6) Bounce ideas off staff and students. (Test possibilities.)
(7) Conflict resolution training promises the best results (Choose.)	(8) Implement peer counselor training. (Act.)	(9) Monitor incidents of violence. (Evaluate.)
(10) Routinize conflict resolution training as an ongoing program. (Provide maintenance.)		

- Comfort with risk taking
- A willingness to trust their instincts
- Openness to giving credit to others for contributing to sound decisions

Administrators who want to become better decision makers are well advised to work on honing these traits. Welcoming and even seeking out new opportunities to make tough decisions is the first step.

INTUITIVE LEADERSHIP: WHEN TO TRUST YOUR INSTINCTS

One secret that all effective school leaders learn is that not all decisions are (or can be) based on facts and tangible, verifiable data. Intuition can be a valuable aid to problem solving and decision making as well. Elvis Presley is credited with coming up with the admonition, "Trust your gut. It doesn't know how to lie." Elvis was right! Good decision makers put faith in their instincts.

Not all decisions can be made simply by adding up the pluses and minuses. Sometimes, it pays to trust your hunches. They often have a way of working out. Smart decisions may come from the head, but right decisions often come from the heart. Effective leaders learn to listen to their feelings and are bold enough to follow their heart when it sends out strong messages.

"Does it feel right?" is an important question for decision makers who trust their instincts. Intuitive leaders develop a heightened awareness of circumstances, surroundings, events, and other people's thoughts and feelings as well as their own. Often they pick up subliminal cues and clues that point to the right direction and that most other people miss. By using holistic (cognitive and instinctive) thinking, intuitive leaders also are frequently in a position to allow serendipity to work in their behalf.

Fortunately, intuitive leadership is learnable. (Watch little children. They use intuition all the time.) It's mostly a matter of paying attention to your inner voice and unmasking your true feelings.

The best times to use intuition in decision making are when

- The facts don't add up
- The process is moving along too slowly (or too quickly), and you feel uncomfortable about how it's working out
- Everything seems right, but feels wrong
- There's something about the pending decision that makes you feel vaguely guilty or uneasy

Intuition isn't guesswork; neither is it infallible. It is simply a tool that effective leaders aren't afraid to use to help make a decision when appropriate.

Whether decisions are based on intelligence, input, or intuition, not all of them are going to work out. Every leader sometimes makes a dumb decision. When this happens, the important thing is to accept blame without shame, learn the lessons that failure has to teach, and move on (see Chapter 7, Dealing With Setbacks).

Deciding stuff is what leaders do. The process is basically the same in all fields. What's different for school leaders is that although they have many choices and decisions to make, they have only one standard to apply: What's best for kids!

2

Planning for the Future

S ome school administrators always seem to be a step ahead of the game. They're customarily cool, confident, and in control. Others seem to be perpetually frazzled, ricocheting through each day and always playing catch-up. What's the difference? Often, the answer is that one has a plan, and the other doesn't have a clue. Leadership is more than a series of knee-jerk reactions.

Too many administrators think that planning is something they'll do when they have time. They never do. One of the secrets of successful leaders in all fields is that they plan to have time to plan.

Having a plan, even a flawed one, is better than having no plan at all. With a plan, you may end up where you want to be. Without one, you can end up anywhere.

Leadership and planning go together. Leaders plan—period! They don't wait for time to plan. They don't complain about not having time for planning. They don't make excuses for not planning. They simply and systematically set aside time to dream about the future, envision possibilities, project and extrapolate, predict, set goals, outline strategies, and establish time lines. That's called planning. It's what all good leaders do. To become an effective principal, superintendent, or other school leader, you need to be a chronic planner. It's not as difficult as you may think.

THE PLANNING HABIT

Successful school leadership is never random. It is purposeful by nature. That requires planning. Conscious preparation and planning are the only antidotes for organizational drift.

The surest way to move beyond perfunctory school management to a higher level of leadership is to make planning a priority. That means planning each day every day and planning for your school's future at the same time. Planning works. It's fun. It's habit forming. It's one of the secrets of effective leadership in any field.

The following tips can help you make planning a habit:

1. Save time for reflection and planning every day. Make it routine.

2. Find a comfortable place both at home and at work that is conducive to thinking and planning. (It doesn't have to be your office.) Remember, silence is a friend of planning.

3. Establish a no-interruption rule during planning time.

4. Use downtime as planning time. There's no rule against making plans during drive time or wait time.

5. Try walking and planning. They often go together.

6. Give yourself a quota (e.g., 10 new ideas for improvement) and a deadline (e.g., complete planning for next semester by the end of the month).

7. Don't be fooled into thinking that planning has to be formal, fancy, or complicated. Keep it comfortable and manageable. Keep it simple. Often, the easiest plan or planning process is best.

8. Let your subconscious do part of your planning for you. Plant the seed. Alert your mind to the plans you're making and then let things incubate for a while. Solutions and innovative ideas sometimes come out of nowhere.

9. Start with questions. What's needed? What's preferred? What's possible? What are the obstacles? What are the odds?

10. Always keep a notebook or recording device handy day and night to record spontaneous planning ideas or inspirations that may come to you at unexpected times.

To establish planning as the way you do business in your school, department, or office, do whatever it takes to have, find, or make time for it on a regular basis. Put it on your calendar and daily planner. Don't apologize for taking time to plan. Convince your secretary or executive assistant that your planning time is important and must be respected. Tell others what you're doing and why. Encourage them to get into the habit as well. Planning can be contagious.

To make it a priority, you may have to change the way you think about planning. The best organizational planning starts with a vision.

HOW EFFECTIVE SCHOOL LEADERS USE THE VISIONING PROCESS

The Bible admonishes that "Without a vision, the people will perish." Good leaders know that it's true. Planning the future begins and ends with a vision.

Holding a clear-cut image of what the organization can become is one of the key factors that separates leaders from mere school managers. Vision is a true leader's stock in trade. (In most unstructured groups, the person with the best vision gets to be the leader.) If a superintendent or principal can define, articulate, and "sell" a specific image of tomorrow, that image will, in fact, become the future.

Don't make the mistake of always being too busy to get around to visioning and planning. Your choice is to envision the future you want for your school, department, or office and to work toward it—or to become a victim of a future you never intended and had no hand in designing.

Likewise, never be afraid of being labeled a "visionary." The term sometimes gets a bad rap. It merely means a person who looks ahead. Where else would you expect a leader to look? A vision is essential to helping you filter options and drive decision making. The truth is that it's hard to be anything more than a manager without some mental picture of the kind of operation you want to lead. If you want to become a leader, work on building a vision of what a good organization looks like and how it behaves. Reminding yourself of why you became an educator in the first place is a good way to start in designing your own personal vision of the future.

Fortunately, a viable vision doesn't have to be ethereal, complicated, radical, or revolutionary. It doesn't even have to be original or completely different from all other visions. It just has to be positive, somewhat uplifting, worthwhile, challenging, understandable, attainable, appropriate to the time and place, acceptable to most stakeholders, and custom-fit to your organization. It also helps if the vision contains some elements of fun and excitement.

There's no reason to be intimidated by the visioning process. You can do this. It can even be one of the most rewarding dimensions of leadership.

Whenever a leader and others in the school organization agree on a shared vision and write it down, it becomes their mission statement. Most successful entities have one. If yours doesn't, think about it.

A mission statement is simply the dream of the school or school system reduced to writing. It spells out what the organization is about, how it differs from others, and what it hopes to become. It makes you accountable on paper.

Sample School Mission Statements

The purpose of _____ School, as the cornerstone of a lifelong learning community, is to make all learners academically prepared, self-reliant, curious, thoughtful of others, and capable of using their learning to succeed in life in an interdependent world.

Our mission is to provide a

> Caring
>
> Environment for
>
> Lifelong learning that
>
> Enhances self-concept and
>
> Broadens social and scholastic skills by
>
> Responding to our changing society so that
>
> All learners survive and
>
> Thrive with
>
> Excellence

A good mission statement serves as the foundation for all future planning. It helps sort out alternatives and guide choices. Mission statements come in all sizes and shapes (see the sample mission statements below). Although shorter is usually better, the important thing is that the mission accurately explains why the organization exists and what it intends to accomplish.

Effective leaders use their mission statement to stay focused and to keep them honest while planning for the future. Other uses include helping leaders to allocate resources, prioritize tasks, clarify issues, manage time, motivate staff, channel energies, stay grounded, and remain humble. With all of these applications, it's easy to see why a well-honed vision and/or mission statement can be a leader's most valuable tool.

No vision or mission statement is complete unless it is backed up by a well-defined set of commonly held beliefs. All organizations (including schools) become what they believe. It's always important that everyone involved know what these beliefs are. People can't connect or commit if they don't know what the school or school system stands for.

Every leader has an obligation to shape and articulate the belief system of the organization. These beliefs constitute what's valued, rewarded, allowed, and prized within the system.

The strongest belief statements are defined by consensus. The most common means of reaching consensus on beliefs is to use a "forced choice" approach whereby all suggestions are noted and then systematically retained or eliminated by having all stakeholders indicate their top priorities until the list is reduced to a workable size.

Sample School Belief Statements

In these we believe:

- **Success**—All people can learn, and learning should be lifelong. Everyone should experience success and be duly recognized. Such success is essential to self-actualization and development of a positive self-concept. Our goal is a program and learning environment that yields "zero rejects."

- **Excellence**—We believe that our school has achieved excellence and can achieve eminence. Our goal is to be the best we can be.

- **Service**—The whole community is our customer, and our sole purpose is to serve. Thus, we value parental and community involvement. Getting along with people is the single most important talent we bring to our profession.

- **Empowerment**—We believe in empowering people, decentralizing decision making, and fostering opportunities for growth for all students and staff.

- **Culture**—The culture of the organization is an important variable that should be nurtured and celebrated in order for our schools to be healthy, happy, and productive places to live and learn.

- **Teamwork**—We are each other's greatest strength, and all are accountable for organizational outcomes. Collaboration, congeniality, open communication, caring, listening, and loyalty are essential to the success of our schools.

- **Evaluation**—Evaluation should drive instruction to meet individual student needs and maximize mastery learning. Effective evaluation and the proper use of results can enable us to reallocate limited resources to accomplish desired goals.

- **The Future**—We have a positive view of the future and believe we can create such a future. It is our job to model this belief for our students, our community, and ourselves.

(The belief statements above have been adopted by the St. Louis Park Public Schools in Minnesota.)

Another popular consensus-reaching technique is to use an "affinity diagram," which organizes suggestions into clusters based on similarities and common themes. Stakeholders then select the most representative idea from each cluster.

Belief statements, like mission statements, help focus team efforts on what is important and serve as a constant reminder of what counts in the organization. Planning then becomes mostly a manner of finding ways to get staff to act on their beliefs. For this purpose, many school leaders find it helpful to write down and publicize the beliefs, as in the sample list above.

Whether they are formal or informal (written or unwritten), the organization's vision, mission, and belief statements should be the basis for all subsequent individual and group planning efforts. They especially provide the superstructure for long-range strategic planning, which affects the entire system.

STRATEGIC PLANNING BY THE NUMBERS

Strategic planning is scary to many educators. It sounds too technical, scientific, and sophisticated. It's something CEOs and corporations do; but we don't have time for that sort of thing in the public school. Wrong!

Strategic planning doesn't have to be complicated. It's just another fancy name for systematic, long-range planning. (Actually, it's not even that long range—usually 3–5 years. Anything longer is too speculative.)

A more down-to-earth definition of strategic planning is simply "writing down your expectations for the organization and then meeting those expectations." An even better definition might be the following: "creating a sequence of events that leads to desired ends." Managers never have time for this kind of planning. Leaders always do.

Strategic planning is a way of inventing the future. Lots of things will happen to your organization over the next 3 to 5 years. You can wait for things to happen, you can just let things happen, or you can make things happen. Strategic planning is an effective leader's way of making sure that the right things happen.

Tomorrow is something that can be shaped and influenced today. Whatever happens to your organization in the years ahead will have been created, prompted, or allowed by what you and your staff do or don't do today. Schools and school systems can alter their destinies through advance planning. If you don't consciously plan a future for your organization, others (including politicians, business leaders, and special interest groups) will do it for you.

Visions don't materialize into reality on their own volition. Hard work is required to map out and implement strategies to achieve desired outcomes. (The best part of any dream is making it happen.) That's what strategic planning is for.

Every effective leader in any field today has to be a strategic planner. The good news is that it's not overly difficult. The essence of strategic planning is simply analyzing the current state of the organization measured against its vision of the future and finding ways to get from here to there. It is basically a process of identifying long-range targets and spelling out what it takes to hit them. In this way, the planning process can be a source of revitalization for the entire organization.

Too many school managers view strategic planning as an onerous paper-and-pencil exercise in futility. Winning administrators, however, realize that it is a real-world form of leadership in action. A simple strategic planning process can be cleansing, healthy, and renewing for the organization and everyone in it. That's leadership!

There's no right or wrong way to do strategic planning, but most experienced planners follow a common pattern. If you want to initiate and implement strategic planning by the numbers, here are the steps to follow:

Strategic Planning Steps

1. Define the mission (the future vision of the organization).

2. Do an external (environmental) scan.

3. Review current societal trends and project future needs.

4. Do an internal scan.

5. Review strengths and weaknesses within the organization. Pay special attention to potential threats, possible allies or partners, and existing sacred cows and taboos embedded in the culture of the organization. All stakeholders should have an opportunity to participate in this review process.

6. Identify preferred long-range key results (measurable outcomes).

7. Rank desired results and set priorities.

8. Develop an implementation plan.

9. Develop strategies. Sequence events. Identify resources. Assign responsibilities. Establish timetables.

10. Implement the action plan.

11. Monitor progress.

12. Track progress toward achieving each key result.

13. Keep all stakeholders informed of hits and misses.

14. Review and renew the plan.

15. Subject the plan to periodic reality checks and relevancy tests. Modify and adjust it as needed. Renew your effort.

In addition to these steps, some educational leaders are now introducing a new wrinkle into the traditional strategic planning process.

One weakness of many school plans is that the outcomes are stated in terms of what teachers and others will do for and with students. The real focus should be on what happens to the students themselves. What is missing is a learner impact statement.

Just as the federal government requires an environmental impact statement before major projects are undertaken, some schools see a need to define the precise impact on learners of every new practice or program under consideration. Adding a learner impact statement can sharpen the focus of planning, provide one more reality check, and put some discipline into the exercise of translating theory into practice.

Learner Impact Form

Key Result: _____

Target Learners: _____

1. What will the target students be able to perform, achieve, or do better because of this key result?

2. What other benefits will target students realize because of this key result?

3. How will this key result adversely affect the target students?

4. What other problems for students or others may be created by this key result?

5. What quantifiable outcome measure will be used to document this key result's impact on learners?

6. What other means of evaluation will be used to measure the learner impact of this key result?

Name: _____ Title: _____ Date: _____

(Please attach any supporting material or data.)

Stakeholder's Input Form

Please respond to the questions below:

A. Are there school initiatives, programs, or priorities that should be receiving less attention or dropped? If so, list them.

B. What, if any, new results should the school seek to achieve in the next 3 to 5 years?

C. The foregoing suggestions are a result of (check one)
_____ Group consensus   _____ Individual recommendation

Strategic reforms and innovations that merely sound good to the public or that make the adults feel like they're trying simply aren't good enough. The litmus test is, do they benefit kids?

A learner impact statement can supply a heretofore missing piece in the planning process. It helps define the specific effect that the school's strategic plan may have on the learners involved. The learner impact form above shows how it works.

It's important to remember that strategic planning isn't just for the leader. It's for everyone—particularly for the students.

Although each of the steps above (including the learner impact statement) contributes to the process, the real key to successful strategic planning is the widespread involvement of all stakeholders.

Throughout the planning process, participants should be encouraged to practice divergent thinking. It helps to ask trigger questions such as: What else can we do? What other approaches can we use? How else can we achieve this key result?

Once a strategic plan is in place, stakeholders from every level of the organization can set individual and group goals to help implement it.

THE "SMART" MODEL FOR GOAL SETTING

Goal setting is the most simple and common form of planning. Unfortunately, many administrators don't fully appreciate its power. Goal setting can change lives and careers. Effective leaders know this. Many managers don't.

Goals get people going. They provide intrinsic, cost-free motivation—because reaching a goal is its own reward. Goals serve as personal incentives for individuals and groups to make incremental changes for the better. If you are not continuously setting and resetting goals for yourself and your organization, you're something less than a leader.

Goals have built-in power because they are promises we make to ourselves to be and do better. They work best if they are written down and revisited regularly. By asking yourself "How am I doing on my goals?" you can take personal inventory on an ongoing basis.

The best goals excite, inspire, and contain an element of fun. It helps if they build on existing strengths. Many planning consultants, such as Jerry Lebediker of the Performance Management Corporation, recommend using a "SMART" model for setting goals.

Of course, establishing goals can be just blowing smoke (like many New Year's resolutions) or it can mean an exciting new beginning. The difference lies in the degree of commitment and individual will to carry out the goals. Good leaders have a lot of both.

Goal setting can be an important survival tool. If you want to have maximum impact as a school leader, you'll take it seriously and use it as part of an overall planning cycle.

SMART Goals

Goals should be

S–Specific (well defined)
M–Measurable (so you can gauge progress)
A–Action oriented
R–Realistic (challenging but doable)
T–Time oriented (include deadlines)

An example of one such goal is the following: As part of the school's efforts to eliminate student "bullying," we will develop and teach a 4-hour unit titled "Respect" to all second graders beginning in October 2005.

This example meets the SMART criteria: It is specific (a 4-hour unit), measurable (all second graders), action oriented (we will develop and teach), realistic (doable with existing school resources), and time oriented (beginning in October 2005).

A FLOWCHART FOR EFFECTIVE PLANNING

Visioning, strategic planning, and goal setting shouldn't be episodic. They need to be cyclical and require continuous efforts in order to be effective. Planning works only if it relentlessly moves the organization in the direction of its dream.

The following chart illustrates how all of the steps in the process can flow together in an uninterrupted pattern of choosing and rechoosing the future (see Exhibit 2.1).

Planning isn't something done intermittently. For most effective leaders, planning is an attitude and a way of doing business every day. Where it works best, plans are constantly reviewed, revised, and recycled.

PLANNING IS A SECRET WEAPON

Some readers may think this chapter makes too big a fuss about planning. After all, who has time for all this visioning, strategic planning, and goal setting? The answer is just about every effective leader you have ever known or heard about.

Planning of any kind is essentially a form of preparation, and preparation is the first step toward success in any field.

Remember the Boy Scout motto, "Be prepared"? No matter what you think of the organization, you have to admire the motto.

Most of today's school leaders grew up learning about the power of preparation. They heard all the stories about actors and athletes preparing themselves for years. They knew that most Hollywood overnight successes were the results of decades of planning and preparation. They understood Benjamin Franklin's classic admonition, "By failing to prepare we prepare to fail."

Exhibit 2.1   Effective Planning Flowchart

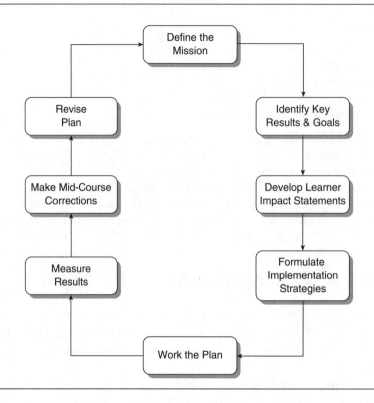

Unfortunately, somewhere along the way, some principals and super-intendents forget how critical planning and preparation are to continued peak performance. Of course, it's true that the more experienced school leaders become, the less time they have to spend planning and preparing. It's only natural. It's OK.

But some veteran school officials cut back on preparation and planning time too soon, too much, and too often. A few try to cut it out altogether. That's not leadership. It's planning to fail. (Remember Ben Franklin?)

Of course, beginners have to prepare more than seasoned administra-tors. But the need to plan carefully and prepare fully never completely goes away. It should be no surprise that there are principals and superin-tendents who think they're good enough, smart enough, and experienced enough that they don't need to spend much time planning ad preparing for anything. (Have you ever noticed that experience and arrogance go together?) Since they've "been there and done that," they think they can wing it. They're missing an important point: Even champions need to plan and prepare. They just don't make a big deal out of it.

As long as some school administrators don't see their peers doing a lot of planning, they falsely assume that it isn't going on. What they don't know is that it is what they don't see that often spells the difference between winners and losers.

The best in any business are always prepared. One of the best-kept secrets of successful school leadership (or any leadership) is that it takes a lot of planning time to appear spontaneous. The truth is that no matter how long you've been on the job, you never get too good to do careful planning.

Most school leaders are smart, well trained, and hardworking. So what sorts out the best from the rest? You guessed it. At the end of the day, the prize goes to the one who has planned and prepared the best and the most.

Planning provides an edge. It is a secret weapon that some school officials forget, neglect, ignore, downplay, or deny. If you are not planning for every day on the job, you're shortchanging your students, staff, community, and, most importantly, yourself.

It is no coincidence that baseball's Hall of Famers Joe DiMaggio and Ted Williams took more batting practice than all of their teammates combined. They wanted to be better prepared than anyone else on the field. They knew that was the only way to get to the top of their trade—and stay there. It works the same way in school leadership. The Boy Scouts had it right all along.

Of course, it's easy to find reasons to skip or skimp on planning. As I mentioned earlier, the most common rationalization is "I don't have time." Being busy may be an alibi or an explanation, but it is not a valid excuse.

The truth is that no school leader has time to be unprepared. Lack of proper planning or preparation inevitably results in additional time spent reversing, revising, and repairing mistakes or in spin-doctoring and damage control. Planning doesn't waste time, it saves time.

What do star performers plan for? Everything! Champion baseball sluggers never know what pitch is coming next, so they prepare to hit whatever comes. Effective school leaders do the same thing.

For principals and superintendents, every day is different, surprises are normal, and ambushes are just part of doing business. Preparation and planning are the only ways to be proactive, rather than reactive. As a leader, you can manage anything that happens if you've planned for it in advance.

No matter how experienced you are as a school administrator, you still need to plan every day for

- Holding conferences
- Handling confrontations
- Giving pep talks
- Brainstorming solutions
- Disciplining students (and adults)
- Defending positions
- Selling ideas
- Handling crises
- Coordinating efforts
- Responding to questions
- And much more

Obviously, these are all everyday operations. As an administrator, you have done them all before—more than once. But each situation is unique, with different particulars, parameters, possibilities, and nuances. Every upcoming conference, conversation, meeting, or other function deserves its own specific form of planning and preparation. The point is to do whatever it takes to anticipate problems, weigh choices in advance, and plan a variety of responses.

Former New York City mayor Rudolph Giuliani takes it even a step further by urging leaders to instill a "culture of preparedness" throughout the organization. Good school leaders pass the planning ethic on to their entire staff.

According to Giuliani, successful leaders plan and prepare relentlessly. "Preparation is the key to success. . . . Leaders can possess brilliance, extraordinary vision, fate, even luck—but no one can perform without preparation," he adds.

Could the Boy Scouts, Ben Franklin, and Rudy Giuliani all be wrong? Don't bet on it. If you cut down, cut back, or cut out planning for each day on the job, you are depriving yourself of a powerful secret weapon. Success without planning is just "dumb luck." Unfortunately, there isn't enough of that to go around.

PLANNING FOR SUCCESS

Managers spend all their time carrying out other people's plans. Leaders make their own.

The old saw that says "Failing to plan is planning to fail" is more than a cliché—it's reality. If you want to crank up your leadership a notch, become a planning fanatic. Plan in your head. Plan on paper. Plan in private. Plan in public. Just plan. It's one key to continuous improvement and successful leadership.

The power of planning and goal setting isn't limited to just your job and your career. It can work in your personal life as well. The best leaders you know live a balanced life. They have time for work, family, spirituality, their community, themselves, and fun. That doesn't happen by accident. It takes planning.

Another secret of success at work and in life is to always have a backup or contingency plan. Things go wrong. Reversals happen. The unexpected occurs. Any of these developments can wreck your plans unless you have an escape route, an alternative course of action, or a fall-back position. Good leaders are big believers in Plan B.

Whether it's Plan A or Plan B, your plan is your passport to the future. Good plans also help you get the most out of other people and yourself.

3

Getting the Most
Out of People

As long as you're doing most of the work yourself, you're not leading anyone. Administrators stuck in a caretaking manager mode often fall into the trap of doing too much themselves. Real leaders, on the other hand, achieve results by working through others.

In sports, the winningest coaches are those who get the most out of their players. What works with athletic squads can work with school personnel as well. The administrator who can get the maximum effort out of everyone in the organization is always a cut above the rest.

We all know principals and superintendents who consistently bring out the best in everyone. They are able to keep people interested, charged up, focused, and working hard. They know how to get staff and students to want to be and do their best.

How do they do it? It's not magic, but it does take a combination of know-how, style, attitude, artistry, timing, hard work, and attention to detail. Getting the most out of people starts with a leadership style that promotes maximum productivity from everyone.

WINNING AND LOSING LEADERSHIP STYLES

There are about as many leadership styles as there are personality types (and almost as many efforts to categorize and label them). Some styles are open. Some are closed. Some are flexible. Others are more rigid. Some are cognitive. Some are emotive. Some leaders have a style that is manipulative. Others have a more participatory style. Some styles are driven by product and others by process.

The most critical difference separating winning and losing leadership styles among school leaders is where they fall along the spectrum of power use shown below:

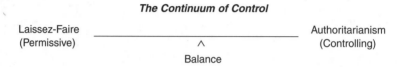

The Continuum of Control

Laissez-Faire   Authoritarianism
(Permissive)   ∧   (Controlling)
                                      Balance

It should come as no surprise that the best leaders align themselves somewhere around the middle of the continuum. They try to balance direction with freedom. Sometimes, they lead people by the hand into the future; other times, they merely point people in the right direction and get out of the way. There are reasons why the middle of the road is the best path to follow.

Laissez-faire leadership is an oxymoron. Allowing too much permissiveness isn't leadership at all—it's chaos. And attempts at autocratic management don't work well with today's independent-minded, unionized, rights-conscious professionals. Authoritarianism only drives resistance underground. The days of leading by executive fiat are long gone.

What works and what doesn't changes over time. Leaders have to change, too. See Table 3.1 for a listing of what's in and what's out in leadership styles today.

Part of the reason that leaders change is that followers change. The modern teacher corps and other employee groups are more assertive and unwilling to be patronized than were school staffs in the past. They ask more "why" questions, expect more entitlements, want to be consulted more, and are more willing to criticize the school organization and its leaders than earlier groups did. They do not respond well to a paternalistic management style.

What works best for school leaders today is a "coach" style that helps people develop their own solutions rather than handing out expert advice. This kind of leadership is based on demonstrated human values, such as truth, trust, mentoring, openness, risk taking, giving credit, sharing blame, honesty, and caring.

Of course, no one leadership style works perfectly all the time. That's why some successful administrators favor an eclectic (situational) approach that uses "whatever works" under the circumstances.

In forming your own leadership style, it pays to step back and look at how you treat and interact with subordinates and how they react to you. If you talk a lot more than you listen, if you're receiving an inordinate

Table 3.1   Today's Leadership Styles

In	*Out*
Accountability	Buck passing
Data-driven decisions	Expediency decision making
Consensus building	Coercion
Accessible leadership	Aloofness and/or separation
Flattened organizational chart	Hierarchical structure (caste system)
Free-flowing information	Secrecy
Team building	Divide and conquer
Building on strengths	Focus on weaknesses
Expectations	Rules
Collegialism	Conformity based on fear
Shared decision making	Centralized decision making
Encouragement	Bullying
Honesty	Game playing
Empowerment	Exploitation
Proactive measures	Reactive responses
Linkages	Turf building
Questioning	Issuing of directives
Informality	Formal structure
Modeling	Telling
Self-disclosure	Executive mystique
Negotiations	Mandates
Compromise	Confrontation
Counseling	Ordering
Open discussion	Pontification
Acceptance of good ideas	Top-down ideas from any source flow
Removing obstacles	Creating hoops
Leader as servant	Leader as superior

number of grievances, or if staff members clam up when you're around or resist bringing you problems, your style may be out of touch.

It also helps to think of the best principals and superintendents you know and to identify what it is about their styles that seems to click with their subordinates. Some of the best sources of worthy role models are state and national professional organizations, such as the National Association of Elementary School Principals (NASP), the National Association of Secondary School Principals (NASSP) and the American Association of School Administrators (AASA). Benefits of participating in professional associations include exposure to new ideas and friendships, opportunities for personal and professional growth, and possibilities for networking with the best in the business. Such ties are particularly crucial to administrators in small or isolated school districts.

Don't be afraid to borrow from the best. There's no copyright law covering leadership styles. It doesn't mean you're becoming phony. It just means you're learning to be a better leader.

Fortunately, your leadership style isn't like DNA. You're not born with it or stuck with it forever. If you don't like your style, or if it's not working, you can change it. You'd better change it!

MORALE: DOES IT MATTER ANYMORE?

Whatever leadership style you adopt will shape and be shaped by the morale of all those working within the organization. Morale influences how you lead, how much you can expect, and how much you really get out of people.

Morale is the cornerstone of productivity in all human organizations. School systems are no exception. Administrators willing to settle for just being managers of things-as-they-are may not have to worry much about morale, but effective leaders do.

We used to hear a lot about morale and school culture. But with all of today's mounting stresses, escalating expectations, rampant school bashing, and pressures to do more with less, does staff morale really matter anymore? You bet it does!

Morale is as important as ever, and yet it's never been lower in many schools (particularly in hard-pressed, inner-city areas). To get the most out of all employees today, it's imperative for school leaders to revisit the issue of teacher, staff, and student morale and to do something about it.

The best definition of *morale* is simply how school staff members and students feel about themselves, their work or studies, their "bosses," their school, and their overall professional or learning life. Good morale results in a strong sense of common purpose, mutual support, and unified effort. Low morale produces noncommittal attitudes, half-hearted efforts, and lackluster performances. No school or school system can be better than how the people in it feel about it.

Morale is the catalyst that brings together all of the human elements in the organization and produces results. With high morale, school personnel work hard, have fun, and reach their goals (and then some). In situations where morale is low, nobody tries and nobody cares. Accomplishment becomes an embarrassment.

Leaders determine good or bad morale more than any other single factor. Cultivating a positive, productive school culture and climate is the real work of real leaders. If you don't think it's your business, you'd better stick with being a caretaker manager. You're missing the point of leadership.

The first step in managing morale is to gauge the existing state of feelings for and about the organization. Administrators often don't like to recognize or admit morale problems because the problems might reflect on their own effectiveness. Nevertheless, it's always better to identify problems and deal with them up front than it is to ignore them and let them get worse through neglect. Denial is not a successful leadership technique.

Assessing morale isn't rocket science. Even casual visitors can often pick up positive and negative vibes and give a pretty accurate appraisal of the state of morale. You know you have high morale when people like to come to school, show up fresh every morning, laugh and have fun together, care about the image of the organization, tackle even hard tasks willingly, show pride in the school, and even go the extra mile to achieve established goals.

It's equally easy to spot serious morale problems in the making. You usually don't need to spend a lot of money on sophisticated studies or research. An informal audit will tell you all you need to know about existing morale in most cases (see the sample "Morale Audit" below).

Whether morale is good or bad, there's always work for effective leaders to do. Low morale can be turned around. Good morale can get even better. Often, the administrator in charge is the only one who can make things improve.

For starters, below are 15 school-tested strategies that you can put to use today to upgrade morale and get more out of people:

1. Admit mistakes.

2. Promote from within.

3. Respect privacy.

4. Help beginners.

5. Praise in public, criticize in private.

6. Be consistent. (Staff and students shouldn't have to guess which leader is going to show up.)

7. Give honest feedback on a regular basis.

8. Listen—a lot!

9. Create opportunities for professional and personal growth.

10. Conduct exit interviews to identify problems.

11. Avoid hip-pocket decisions that disregard staff members' feelings or concerns.

12. Get to know staff members better.

13. Make seeking input a habit.

14. Avoid favoritism. Treat everyone alike—fairly.

15. Celebrate together.

Spending time nurturing morale and improving the overall organizational culture and climate is always a cost-effective way to get the most out

Informal Morale Audit: Signs of a Deteriorating Climate

Instructions: Check all that apply.

_____ Absenteeism is high.

_____ Student failures are up.

_____ Buildings and grounds are littered and unkempt (and nobody cares).

_____ Violence is commonplace.

_____ Police calls are up.

_____ Everyone keeps their doors closed (and locked).

_____ Bitching is the norm.

_____ Lounge talk is almost always negative.

_____ There's not much laughter anymore.

_____ Rules are piling up.

_____ No one volunteers.

_____ Language is deteriorating. (Profanity is the idiom of choice.)

_____ Cliques are the most common way to relate.

_____ Vandalism is increasing.

_____ Disrespect is the norm.

_____ Nobody from the district office wants to visit anymore, but union reps are frequent visitors.

_____ Faces are grim. (Where have the smiles gone?)

_____ Substitutes are hard to get.

_____ Everyone leaves as soon as possible.

_____ Bad-mouthing among employees is common.

_____ Public criticism is on the rise.

_____ Transfer requests are growing.

_____ Property values around the school are going down. ("For Sale" signs are common sights.)

Scoring: Even one check is too much.

of people. It's the kind of stuff that successful leaders like to make a priority. Morale building continues to be a trademark of effective leadership.

SHAPING A SCHOOL CULTURE
THAT WORKS FOR EVERYONE

The best school leaders know that morale is largely a function of the school's culture. Yet, many administrators don't understand the concept of "culture" or even know what it is. A few well-meaning principals and superintendents still think of culture strictly as highbrow art and music. Or as a glob of microplasm that medical researchers study under a microscope in a sterile laboratory somewhere. They don't think of culture as any part of their life on the job.

But the truth is that the culture of the school is more important to morale, productivity, teamwork, and success than salaries, benefits, and working conditions are. More than anything else, the culture defines the success or failure of the organization.

Every group or organization (e.g., family, clan, neighborhood, street gang, bridge club, business, labor union or—yes—even a public school) has its own unique culture that defines what's expected, what's accepted, what's preferred, what's tolerated, what's rewarded, what's punished, and what's taboo within the group.

The culture is the "personality" of the school. It is made up of all the mores, core values, cherished beliefs, priorities, traditions, informal rules, roles, and rituals of the organization.

If you want to know who has the real power, how things really get done and what it takes to go along and get along in the school, you won't find the answers in the school rules, union contract, policy manual, or employee handbook. The only way to learn these things is to understand how the culture of the school actually operates.

Unfortunately, there are some administrators who spend their entire career completely unaware of how things really work. They come to work every day without a clue about what's going on around them. It's almost as if they lived and worked in some parallel universe, rather than in the real world of the school.

Naturally, school officials who are out of touch with the culture of the organization quickly become irrelevant. They don't lead the staff. Instead, the employees merely tolerate them and pretty much do things their own way. Does that sound like any schools you know of?

As leader, if you don't have a handle on the culturally embedded behaviors, biases, and beliefs of the staff, you are deprived of a powerful tool for motivating them.

It is the culture on the job that determines how people interact, how they treat each other, how they communicate and what they communicate, how open and honest they will be, how hard they will work, and how much they will put up with.

Likewise, it is the culture that often attracts people to the organization—or drives them away. In most cases, good teachers and other employees don't leave a school because of low pay, large workloads, or lack of resources. They leave because they don't like the culture.

Some cultures are terminally toxic. You've seen schools where no one is willing to be accountable and responsible, where no one seems to care anymore, and where everyone looks tired and worn out. ("You can walk in the door and quickly feel fatigue. They look tired and act tired. There's no sense of urgency," writes John R. Graham, president of Graham Communications, about "tired" organizations.)

The toxic culture of these schools doesn't happen by accident. What makes them that way? Usually, it's the person in charge.

More than anyone or anything else, administrators shape and mold their school culture. Of course, school leaders can't dictate or mandate a particular culture; but they can nudge, cajole, convince, and lead by example. Effective principals and superintendents set a tone for the school by reminding people at all levels of their mission, defining lofty goals, articulating expectations, raising standards, rewarding preferred behaviors, and modeling desired actions and attitudes.

By influencing staff beliefs and behaviors, school leaders can literally create the kind of culture they want for their school. It's not easy. It takes time and hard work; but it is possible and eminently worthwhile.

School cultures are organic and interactive. They are constantly growing, morphing, reforming, adjusting, and adapting. Cultures can change. And principals and superintendents can change them. It's something you can do, too.

The best school leaders strive to create a climate that empowers individual self-actualization and promotes optimum creative collaboration at the same time. The goal is to align the everyday culture of the school with the overall goals of the organization. When that occurs, look out world—big things are about to happen.

If you build that kind of culture in your school, the best teachers will come. They will stay. They will produce. And you will have made your school a better place to work and learn.

The most powerful way to get the most out of all your people and to promote effective teamwork at the same time is to create a school culture that works for everyone. That's what good school leaders do. You don't want to do any less.

IS TEAMWORK ALL IT'S CRACKED UP TO BE?

More and more school leaders (as well as leaders in all fields) are finding that teaming is a powerful key to improved morale and increased productivity.

For too long, teaching has been an isolated profession. Now we know that when teachers team up, supplement, support, assist, challenge, excite, energize, and stretch each other, they offer students a broader perspective than they were able to before teaming.

In fact, teamwork increases output among all levels of school personnel. As part of a team, staff members tend to work harder than they do as individuals. Teams unleash the creative powers of people and make them feel better about themselves. That's a morale booster all by itself.

That's why effective leaders continually look for new and creative possibilities for teaming. They know that teamwork is definitely all it's cracked up to be—and more!

There are some cautions, however. Not every pair or group constitutes a workable team. Successful teams are made up of individuals who have compatible personalities, want to work together, and share common goals. Good teamwork doesn't occur automatically. Teams, like individuals, need practice before they can perform at their optimum level of proficiency and productivity.

Of course, it's possible to get carried away with teaming. Some principals and superintendents start forming teams just for the sake of teaming. That's not leadership—it's mismanagement.

Teams are not a panacea or cure-all. Teams of classroom teachers should be formed only when doing so benefits students, not for the convenience of adults. Interdisciplinary teams often prove to be the most exciting and imaginative.

Outside of the classroom, the best time to double up effort on a problem or project by forming a team is when one party is overloaded, one party can't solve the problem alone, and/or when multiple perspectives are required.

When considering the use of teams as a tool for achieving peak performance, leaders need to know what a successful team looks like. Here are what most veteran administrators agree are common characteristics of effective teams:

- Individuals participate because they want to.
- Individual team members are self-starters.
- All members are accountable.
- Leadership within the team is shared.
- Everyone actively participates and contributes.
- Team members are mutually supportive.
- Expectations are clearly understood.
- Members value diversity and take pride in each other's contributions.
- Loyalty is taken for granted.
- Participants find identity in the group's achievement.
- Members are willing to sacrifice personal recognition for group rewards.

- All parties understand their respective roles on the team.
- Everyone listens and shares information freely.
- The best teams operate informally.
- Team members get along outside of work as well as on the job.

When introducing teaming, school officials need to be patient and willing to scrap an unsuccessful project without abandoning the concept. Other ways that administrators can ensure team success are to (a) offer clear-cut support from the top down; (b) provide necessary training and resources; (c) set boundaries; (d) define expectations; (e) establish a trusting atmosphere; and (f) reward the entire unit, not individual members.

Teaming doesn't deliver miracles, but it is an effective way to multiply individual strengths, pool talents, and get more out of existing staff. Teamwork proves that the whole can be greater than the sum of its parts. It's too good a deal for effective leaders to pass up.

HOW TO GET THE MOST OUT OF STUDENTS

Any manager can carry out a prescribed curriculum, monitor attendance, dish out discipline, see that the buses run on time, and keep the building clean. It takes a real leader, however, to move beyond these routine functions to guarantee that *all* students have a chance and are set up for success. It's the leader's job to remove obstacles and meet student needs so that all learners can do their best and be their best.

Kids today need what students have always needed: structure, discipline, challenge, respect, recognition, chances, choices, second chances, amnesty, and tough love. Finding ways to satisfy these needs is what educational leadership is all about.

It's complicated because students are driven by a different agenda today than they were in the past. The fears, dreams, and concerns of today's children and youth differ from those of previous generations of learners.

Formerly, students were primarily concerned about issues regarding dating, social life, shopping, college and career choices, marriage, and child-rearing. Today, other worries, such as violence, drugs, gangs, and AIDS, compete for their attention.

This new agenda of youth issues makes it trickier to get the most out of students, but it's not impossible. Maximum student achievement is still attainable.

Besides hiring super teachers, the easiest, best, and quickest way to get students to do their best is to expect the best. Positive expectations can transcend all barriers. Raising the bar and establishing higher standards sets in motion a self-fulfilling prophecy that can transform the school. Expect more, get more. It's that simple.

It takes courage to make excellence the only acceptable standard, maintain zero tolerance for failure, deny the notion of throwaway kids, and refuse to accept second best. That's why many managers fall short. They don't teach guts in graduate school. You have to develop them on your own. It happens by consistently doing the right thing despite resistance and against the odds. It's worth it to make a difference for all students.

Thanks to the Minneapolis-based Search Institute, getting the most out of students is no longer a matter of guesswork. For the first time, we now really know how to do it.

Through its breakthrough research of the 1990s, Search identified 40 crucial developmental assets that all students need in order to achieve their full potential and avoid at-risk behaviors such as use of tobacco, alcohol, and drugs. The more of these assets a child or teenager has, the more likely he or she is to succeed in school and in life.

The assets pinpointed by Search have consistently proved nationwide to be essential building blocks in young people's successful growth and development, as well as powerful shapers of their lives and choices. The assets are concrete, positive (internal and external) experiences and qualities that fall into eight broad experience categories: (a) support, (b) empowerment, (c) boundaries and expectations, (d) constructive use of time, (e) commitment to learning, (f) positive values, (g) social competencies, and (h) positive identity.

Examples of the life-altering assets include the following:

- Family support
- Caring neighborhoods
- Caring school environments
- Parent involvement in school
- Adult role models
- Family, school, and neighborhood boundaries
- Constructive time at home
- School engagement
- Bonding to school
- Resistance skills
- Sense of purpose
- Positive view of personal future

(For more information on asset-building research, contact the Search Institute, 700 S. Third Street, Suite 210, Minneapolis, MN 55415.)

Possessing these assets can protect kids from making scary choices. Unfortunately, the Search data show that the average student has only 18 of the 40 assets needed for optimum growth and development. This makes rebuilding the assets in young people the greatest challenge for getting the most out of today's students.

Effective school leaders can truly have a lasting impact by heading up efforts in and out of school to put children first and to promote asset building throughout the community. If you're serious about getting the most out of students, study the research and make the most of it. It's another way to prove to yourself and others that you're much more than a hold-the-line manager.

HOW TO GET THE MOST OUT OF STAFF

Some seasoned administrators believe that the best way to get the most out of students is simply to get the most out of staff. They may be right. Fortunately, what works with kids (e.g., high expectations, respect, fair treatment, etc.) works with adult staff members as well.

One way to promote peak performance from all staff members is to analyze why personnel frequently fail. It helps to know that some of the most common reasons that teachers and other school employees fail are boredom, lack of challenge, limited opportunities for growth, lack of respect, "cog mentality" (powerlessness—feeling like a lowly cog in the machinery of a vast organization), low standards (toleration for sloppy work), inferior and ineffective coworkers, poor working conditions, and lack of leadership (poor supervision).

It bears repeating that part of a leader's job is to remove obstacles. If you take away the excuses for not producing, you will have gone a long way toward getting the most out of faculty and other staff members. But that's not enough.

Your success as a leader who gets the most from people won't depend on your title, your degrees, or your previous experience. It won't be the result of how much you know, how hard you work, what long hours you keep, or anything you say. It will rest almost totally on the way you treat people.

The nurturing and development of subordinates is the key to organizational excellence. The secret is to give what you like to get. Manager types often don't know this. That's why many never become bona fide leaders.

The surest route to productivity is through an unflinching emphasis on high expectations and relentless encouragement. Staff members need to know that the administration believes in them and stands ready to marshal all available resources to help them succeed. Once they are convinced, they will give their best.

How does such a proactive process of constant encouragement manifest itself in the daily operation of the school? What does it all mean on Monday morning? Following are 15 specific ways that you can model, coach, coax, and encourage peak performance from every staff member every day:

1. Set challenging goals and reasonable deadlines. (Your best performers will always respond positively to pressure.)

2. Give full credit for effort and achievement. Be quick to praise. Don't be afraid to give hard workers a little more credit than they deserve.

3. Always allow staff members to participate in making decisions that affect them and their work.

4. Be open, honest, and up front. Keep everyone informed about what's going on—good and bad. Give reasons for your actions.

5. Shred the policy manual if possible. Keep rules few and simple. Professionals need challenge, opportunity, and a vote of confidence, not more rules and regulations.

6. Champion lifelong learning. Give staff members (not just teachers) all the training they want (and maybe a little bit more).

7. Demonstrate absolute integrity and uncompromising fairness. Keep promises. Keep your word. Keep confidences.

8. Celebrate. Have fun at work. Make playfulness part of the daily routine. Enjoy humor. Laugh at yourself. (Others will be laughing at you anyway.)

9. Manage while walking around (MWWA). Get out of the office. Be accessible. Be everywhere. (It's what employees say they want most.)

10. Inspire your staff. Show them what's possible. Give them a vision of what they can become. Some successful leaders do this by applying what popular business columnist Chuck Martin calls the "Law of Expanding Urgency." His principle simply states that employees feel compelled to match the pace of their leader. ("The speed of the leader determines the rate of the pack."—Unknown). The more the boss works with a sense of urgency, the more everyone else is forced to do the same. Sometimes, leadership is merely a matter of picking up the pace.

11. Give second chances. (You may want one yourself sometime.)

12. Be a family-friendly leader. Realize that teachers and other staff members have a life outside of school. ("People work to live, not live to work."—Anonymous). Respect family time. Let employees leave work to attend their children's school events. Let employees do what they have to do in times of family crisis. Model a balanced life. Take time to fulfill your own family obligations.

13. Dare to practice self-disclosure and get to know more about your staff members' lives. Show your human side. Employees like to work for a real person, not an automaton.

14. Delegate responsibilities. Let people grow by taking on additional tasks (see Table 3.2).

15. Focus on winners. Spend time nurturing your superstars and improving marginal employees. Don't spend needless time on the bottom 15% of performers who will never make it. ("Don't water your weeds."—Peter Lynch).

Table 3.2   Do's and Don'ts of Delegating

Do	Don't
Delegate doable tasks that stretch and challenge	Set up an employee for failure
	Delegate only "dirty work"
Define tasks and spell out expectations clearly	Give responsibilities without authority
	Wait too long
Provide needed resources	Keep looking over the delegatee's shoulder
Answer all questions	
Get out of the way	Dictate how a task is to be done
Give feedback	Take back a task (except in an emergency)
Celebrate success	

Expecting good things from staff members and encouraging their efforts doesn't mean coddling them. Good leaders are tough leaders (tougher than some managers dare to be).

Tips on Constructive Criticism

Anyone can nitpick, nag about, take cheap shots at, attack, or tear down another's performance, but constructive criticism gets better results. These tips can help:

- Criticize behavior, not personalities.

- Criticize in private.

- Base criticism on firsthand observation, not on rumors, innuendos, or allegations.

- Be specific; cite real-world examples.

- Stick to facts.

- Stress positive behaviors.

- Acknowledge improvements.

- Offer to help.

Effective leaders don't back away from holding up challenging expectations and rigid standards. They work hard to support hard work. They praise real results. (False praise is as hollow as a false promise.) They evaluate honestly and don't hesitate to criticize when necessary. Practicing encouragement doesn't require walking on eggs.

Done properly, performance evaluation can be a powerful tool for getting the most out of people. Done incorrectly, it can ruin supervisory relationships and undermine effective leadership.

Analyzing another professional's overall performance requires skills that can be learned. Conducting successful evaluations is an art that needs to be perfected over time through practice. Good leaders don't judge or compare performances of diverse staff members hastily. It takes time and exposure (breadth of experience) to build reliable standards of behavior and productivity.

Meaningful evaluations give candid feedback, pinpoint areas for improvement, reinforce good work, and nail down strategies for remedying weaknesses and building on strengths. Never write a performance review or go into an evaluation conference without a specific goal in mind. If you want to make the most of performance appraisals, here are the rules to follow:

- Separate facts from opinions. Clearly identify each.
- Don't get hung-up on extraneous characteristics (e.g., appearance, mannerisms, personality quirks). The important consideration is whether or not the employee produces desired results.
- Don't be unduly influenced by peaks and valleys in performance. Successful careers aren't made out of isolated events.
- Judge all employees by the same standards.
- Don't hide behind written evaluations. Confront questionable employees face to face.
- Don't let personal feelings (e.g., jealousy, resentment, personality conflicts, old grudges, etc.) enter into any professional performance appraisal.
- Keep notes over time. Don't rely on recall.
- Base evaluations on multiple observations.
- Evaluate only factors that are directly job related.
- Never use an evaluation as a threat or punishment.
- Don't put anything in writing that you wouldn't say to the employee in person.
- Don't evaluate when you're angry.
- Don't beat around the bush or sugarcoat needed criticism. Say what has to be said and move on.

Some leaders today are relying more and more on 360 feedback to appraise and improve professional performance. This approach uses input from everyone within the evaluatee's sphere of operation, including supervisors, subordinates, peers, and students. The goal is to get good information that can be used to make wise choices.

Leaders owe it to all employees to make evaluations as complete, accurate, and fair as possible. It's good for the employee, the evaluator, and the organization, and it's another effective way to get the most out of people.

Productivity is the product of people helping each other to do their best. It starts at the top. Managers know that they aren't paid to be nice to people. They're paid to get results. Effective leaders know it's the same thing.

HOW TO GET THE MOST
OUT OF THE DISTRICT OFFICE,
THE SCHOOL BOARD, AND THE COMMUNITY

Many principals and superintendents struggle to manage the moment-by-moment momentum of their organization. They have their hands full handling home fires. They don't have time to relate any more than they absolutely have to with the outside world. Unfortunately, they're blowing a platinum opportunity.

Effective leaders extend their leadership beyond the school in order to multiply their resources and get all the help and support possible to push their programs over the top.

Some schools always seem to get a lot more than their share of the pie. They consistently receive a disproportionate amount of publicity, special attention, donations, contributions, gifts, pilot programs, grant money, discretionary funds, added staffing, bonus materials, and other perks of all kinds. There's a reason for their embarrassment of riches. It's not luck, it's leadership!

It doesn't take any magic Midas touch to gain an edge in getting the most out of the district office, the school board, the parents, and the community. There are lots of ways to do it wrong. The way to do it right is to follow three simple attention-getting strategies:

1. Become visible beyond the school.

2. Build the home-school partnership.

3. Give the public what it wants.

Visibility and leadership go together. (Can you name any invisible leaders?) The administrator with the greatest positive visibility throughout the community and beyond (scandals don't count) usually gets the gold and other goodies.

To increase your leadership quotient, you need to get out, get known, and get noticed. If the movers and shakers don't know who you are, you're not as good a leader as you could and should be. When people think and talk about good schools, you want to be sure it's your school they think of first.

To use visibility to your greatest advantage, go where the money is. Join the Chamber of Commerce and local service clubs (even if you don't live in the community). Get to know the successful and influential alumni. Find out who the local philanthropists are. Always have a wish list handy. Opportunities come to those who are ready to receive them.

Good leaders are never afraid to market their schools. There are no trophies for false humility. Society is full of school bashers, so school officials need to seize every opportunity to balance the coverage.

The most visible administrators are shameless about telling their story. They let people know all the good things that are going on. They're always available to speak to civic groups and arrange for students to perform at community programs whenever possible. They showcase school talent. They also share their problems and frustrations (without whining). How else can you get public support for desired solutions?

An even better way to promote and publicize your school's programs, accomplishments, and needs is to make friends with the media. Be prolific in providing news tips, current and background information, and press releases. Be available. Answer questions (even the delicate and embarrassing ones). Avoid saying "No comment." Be honest. Return reporters' calls. If you don't know, say so. Rapport and credibility with the media is currency you can cash in when you need it.

Rapport with local, state, and federal legislators is also a valuable commodity. Be your own best lobbyist. Don't be a stranger to lawmakers. They can help you a lot when you go after grants and awards or need special favors.

Attention attracts more attention. Awards, grants, bequests, and gifts attract more of the same. Visibility pays off. Make the most of it.

The second must-do strategy for getting more than your share from outside sources is to build strong linkages to your parent population. No matter how good it is, the school staff can't succeed alone. Schools work only when the home-school partnership works. It's the leader's job to forge that partnership. The way to start is to become an out-and-out radical about parental involvement. Savvy school leaders understand that their real customers are the parents, not the children. The school or school system with the greatest parental support is going to be the most successful and the most likely to get an extra large slice of the pie.

To maximize parental support, do everything possible to get parents in and involved in the school. Act like you invented school volunteers. There's almost nothing that goes on in the school that can't be done by the right volunteer with the right supervision. Most schools today haven't even scratched the surface in using volunteers.

Every volunteer represents another pair of hands to help out and another voice to spread the good word about your school. Don't take volunteers for granted. It pays to pamper them.

Although some administrators don't like to have too many visitors and volunteers around because they fear undue meddling and snooping, the best welcome everyone—the more, the better. Schools can't do business without supportive parents and friends. Good leaders take all the help they can get and ask for more.

If parents won't come to the school, there's nothing wrong with taking the school to the parents. Make home visits and encourage staff to do the same. Some creative leaders even hold classes in local malls periodically so that shoppers, neighbors, and parents can see the school in action. It's also a good idea sometimes to schedule student music concerts out in the neighborhoods.

Volunteer Opportunities in Schools (A Partial List)

Room parent	Accompanist
Crossing guard	Office aide
Minicourse teacher	Referee or umpire
PTA chair	Ticket taker
Driver	Property manager
Mentor	Gymnastics spotter
Junior Great Books leader	Chaperone
Club adviser	Preschool screening helper
School store manager	Piano tuner
Computer aide	Bus stop monitor
Equipment manager	Theme reader
Greeter	Tutor
Costume designer	Library helper
Debate judge	Bus monitor
Party organizer	Caller
Get-out-and-vote volunteer	Advisory council member
Consultant	Book nook chair
Landscape helper	Interpreter
Computer repair person	Task force member
Teacher aide	Test timer
Playground supervisor	Sports team scout
Resource person	Usher
Fundraising volunteer	Prompter
Site council member	Storyteller
Big Brother or Sister	Timer
Block home parent	Crowd control assistant
Volunteer coach	Artist-in-residence

If you want extraordinary support, you have to make extraordinary efforts—pull out all the stops—to connect the home and the school.

The third surefire strategy for getting the most from the community is simply to give the public what it wants. Teach the "basics," including phonics. (That's what parents and other citizens want and understand. It's what you're supposed to have been doing all along anyway.) Pay attention to attendance and discipline. Support parental choice. (The trick is to be sure the right people choose your school.) There's no reason for public school administrators to fear parent choice or voucher programs. Good schools will always attract good students.

Of course, the best way to engage everyone's interest and support is to give them what they want most—test scores. Too many wannabe leaders are afraid of releasing test results. Actually, tests and test results should be the school's best friend. ("What gets measured gets done."—Tom Peters).

If scores are high, the community will take pride and will continue to support successful programs. If results are below par, the public can be rallied to help make them better.

Some uptight school managers see publicizing test scores as a threat. The opposite is true. It's a win-win situation for any leader bold enough to take the initiative in providing all the test information that the citizens want, and maybe even a little bit more.

Too many administrators today shy away from community visibility, parental involvement, public relations, politics, and other outside activities. It's not in their job description. This underscores another key distinction between run-of-the-mill managers and effective leaders. Leaders know that working outside the job description is the only way to get the job done.

At the end of the day, the principal or superintendent who gets the most tangible and intangible support from outside the school will have the greatest success inside the school.

HOW EFFECTIVE LEADERS GET THE MOST OUT OF THEMSELVES

Some men and women who are in charge of schools think that leadership is all about fixing everyone and everything else first, and paying attention to themselves last. Wrong.

As a leader, your most precious resource is yourself. You have to take care of yourself first in order to take care of business later. Getting the most out of yourself is a survival skill for leaders. This means staying healthy, fit, and energetic; living a balanced life; and working smarter.

An ailing leader is a liability. All organizations deserve leaders who can give their best. Anything else is unacceptable.

That's why the first law of leadership is that to do your best, you have to feel your best. If you want to be at the top of your game every day, do what most good leaders do: eat sensibly; exercise enough (walking is always good because you can think, plan, decide, choose, and dream at the same time); get the rest you need; and stay away from tobacco, alcohol, and drugs. Clean living may be boring, but it's the best way to preserve your most important resource. ("If you ruin your body, where will you live?"—Anonymous).

Of course, the state of your physical well-being depends, in part, on the state of your feelings and emotional well-being. This is particularly true of the way you feel about your job. If you hate your work or get burned out from it, you feel lousy and you tend to do a lousy job.

One of the characteristics of effective leaders is that they continually find joy in their jobs. This gives them the energy to energize others. They maintain a positive outlook and avoid burnout by focusing on what's right rather than what's wrong, constantly learning and growing on the job, making friends with problems, picking the right dance partners (associating with winners), keeping their sense of humor, and having a life outside of work.

Living a balanced life is another secret of sustained, successful leadership. If you look at the administrators you admire most, you'll see that most of them make time in their lives for family, friends, faith, fun, and much more. They don't just work all the time.

Workaholism has nothing to do with leadership. Many of the best principals and superintendents refuse to work on weekends, religiously take their vacation time, and put a limit on the amount of work they take home. Leadership is not measured by the number of hours worked—it is measured by the results achieved.

One way to start bringing balance into your life is to put family and personal time on your calendar and daily planner right along with job-related appointments, activities, and events. When you make room on your calendar for your personal life, you've taken the first step to balancing your personal life with your work life.

Many leaders today are also finding that it helps to simplify life. Simplification is catching on with leaders as a means to create a better balance between their inner and outer lives. It's possible for frazzled administrators to find greater inner peace simply by slowing down, spending more time with nature, finding out what they don't want in life, and enjoying each moment.

Unfortunately, it's not easy to live a balanced life in the time allotted. Many administrators feel that they just barely have time to manage the routine of the school, with no time left to lead or to live a full life away from work. Their plate is already full. They're right.

Most school personnel can't work much longer, harder, or faster. But they can work smarter. That's what effective leaders do, and you can, too. It's essential to getting the most out of yourself.

Working smarter usually begins by learning to control the four greatest time wasters for school administrators: (a) paperwork, (b) interruptions, (c) meetings, and (d) procrastination. If you can handle these daily demons, you can easily find the time to be an effective leader and to live your own life as well.

The following "Tip Sheets" offer time-saving, work-smarter techniques that work best for many leaders.

Tip Sheet #1: Taming the Paper Tiger

(Several factors contribute to today's paper crisis: the information explosion, computers, copy machines, governmental red tape, and documentation to avert litigation. Anything you do to attack the problem at these sources will pay off in the long run.)

- Have a trusted assistant screen the paper you have to deal with.

- Don't do any paperwork that someone else can do quicker, better, and easier.

- Handle paper only once.

- Set aside a regular time each day for paperwork.

- Use form letters.

- Don't be afraid to rely on a good ghost writer.

- Don't feel you have to read everything. Much of what crosses your desk isn't worth your time and attention. (They don't call it "junk mail" for nothing.)

- Eliminate excess junk mail by calling the Stop Junk Mail Association (800–827–5549).

- Don't save everything. (When in doubt, throw it out.)

- Purge your files annually.

- Save only one copy of a document. Set limits on how long you save material.

- Use e-mail instead of sending hard copies.

- Use postcards instead of letters for communicating with parents and students.

Tip Sheet #2: How to Minimize Interruption

- Set aside interruption-free time each day.

- Don't make your office too comfortable and inviting for others.

- Face your desk away from the door to discourage casual interruptions.

- Instead of an open-door policy, try a "door ajar" policy.

- Remain standing when visitors drop in.

- Limit small talk.

- Have a predetermined signal to alert your secretary to interrupt an interruption when you need to get back to work.

Tip Sheet #3: How to Make Meetings Work for You

- Call meetings only when needed. (Don't call a meeting just because it's 9 a.m. on Monday.)

- Attend only those meetings where your presence is necessary.

- Always have a specific agenda that includes a starting and ending time.

- Start and end on time—every time.

- Schedule meetings at odd times, such as 8:07 a.m., to make people more time conscious.

Tip Sheet #4: How to Overcome Procrastination

- Establish and announce deadlines.

- Do the most important things first.

- Break big jobs into smaller, manageable parts.

- Give yourself permission to not do a perfect job sometimes. (Some tasks don't deserve perfection.)

- Reward yourself when you complete tough tasks.

Tip Sheet #5: Other "Work-Smarter" Techniques

- Learn when and how to say no and make it stick.

- Hire self-starters who can work with minimal direction and supervision.

- Build flexibility into your daily schedule (e.g., block out more time than is needed for certain appointments, meetings, or activities).

- Question routines and look for ways to streamline bureaucracy.

- Do the right things first.

- Do things right the first time.

- Make prioritizing a priority.

- Don't take on other people's problems.

- Get work done while others aren't around (e.g., early, during lunch hour, and after hours).

- If something isn't working, try something else.

- When you feel overwhelmed, step back, take stock, and start over one step at a time.

If you stay healthy, balance your life, and work smarter, you've done about all you can do to get the most out of yourself. It will be enough, but you won't know that until you try it.

No one facet of leadership takes dramatic precedence over all others, but getting the most out of people (including yourself) comes close. If you can get everyone in the organization producing at a level close to his or her potential, you'll be surprised how much you can change things for the better.

4

Bringing About Change

If a school, school system, or any other organization doesn't want to change anything, it doesn't need much of a leader. A manager will do. Managers try to keep everyone satisfied and contented with the status quo. Leaders aren't afraid to make people uncomfortable enough to want to change.

Of course, both managers and leaders deal with change every day. Managers react to it. Good leaders make it happen. The latter is a lot more challenging, rewarding, and fulfilling. It can also be more frustrating and demanding.

Nevertheless, change is the real currency of leadership. Effective leaders in all fields envision change, show others what is possible through change, and orchestrate change at many levels. Many leaders are hired explicitly to serve as "change agents."

The ability to change things for the better is another mark of true leadership. If you don't want to change anything, you really don't want to be a leader. But if you do want to make a difference through change, you can learn how to do it.

Naturally, change is always scary and difficult—particularly in schools. ("Changing schools is like moving a cemetery."—Anonymous). Unlike many organizations in the private sector, most schools don't have a separate research and development (R&D) department, so they have to change on the wing. Bringing about systemic change in schools is like fixing a bicycle while you're riding it. It's tricky business. That's why adventuresome leaders (there aren't any other kind) like it.

If you want to be good at bringing about worthwhile change, it helps to understand the change process. What is it? How does it work? Who wants it anyway? There are some surprises.

CHANGE: WHO WANTS IT?

In the school business, more than in many other fields, things are not always what they seem to be when it comes to change. If you read the daily newspapers, watch the TV news, or just listen to everyday people talk at social gatherings, you easily get the impression that everybody backs making changes in today's schools. Everyone seems to be clamoring for school reform. The closer you get to making significant change, however, the more you find that appearances are deceiving. Not everyone really wants real change.

Many teachers give lip service to school reform, but deep down, they don't want much to change. They're comfortable where they're at. To make things different might mean making things harder for them. Last year's lesson plans might not do anymore. Teachers have a stake in the present. They don't know what their stake in the future might be if too many changes occur.

Likewise, teacher unions don't normally support significant changes because reforms might infringe on their sovereignty and might place more burdens (work) on their constituents.

Administrators often don't want too much change, either. It usually means more work, and they're already overloaded. Besides, if their teachers don't want it, they don't want it.

Students don't usually want any radical reform, because most proposed changes today involve higher standards, more tests, more requirements, more courses, and/or more time spent in school. Who needs it? Another reason that many students resist reform is that they are much more conservative at heart than most adults think they are. Teens especially want to rebel against existing structures, but they really don't want these structures to be dramatically altered.

Likewise, the majority of parents don't want schools to change significantly. They'd like to keep schools the way they were when they went to school. That's what they understand. You can't count on large numbers of parents to spearhead school reform.

School boards often don't want dramatic change because it usually costs more, and, if it doesn't work, they're left with egg on their elected faces.

Taxpayers commonly oppose change because of added costs. Taxpayers are conservative; change proponents aren't. Taxpayers just want schools to keep doing what they've been doing—only do it better and cheaper.

Legislators and politicians don't want school change unless it makes them look good and the voters support it. The only way that happens is if they compromise on change, which is what legislatures always do.

Many people give lip service to serious change, but who really wants it? In reality, the only people, besides academics, who consistently champion change are vested interest groups that support narrow changes that will benefit them directly. When it comes to change in schools, nobody wants too much of it—except visionary leaders who know that we can do better.

Effective leaders know that change is hard and support is soft, but they don't let that stop them. If they did, they would be stop-gap managers, not true leaders.

Would-be leaders often think that being a change agent is like being a hero. It's not. Change is never as easy or as glamorous as it might appear. It's not about riding the crest of a tidal wave of popular opinion. It's not like leading the charge followed by a cheering band of loyal supporters eager to go wherever you take them. Change isn't heroic. It's hard work. Leaders only do it because it needs to be done.

Successful change requires painstakingly laying a foundation, planning in incredible detail, tediously covering and recovering all the bases, continuously explaining and re-explaining, dealing with naysayers, playing politics, soothing egos, dispelling fears, cheerleading, troubleshooting, communicating, compromising, coaxing, cajoling, and, ultimately, dragging a few stragglers kicking and screaming into the future. That's hard work. It's also leadership.

If you're not up for a fight, you're not up for implementing significant change in schools. You're also not quite up to being an effective school leader yet. The best way to gear up and get up for tackling change is simply to ask, "What happens if we don't?"

The first thing to learn about change is that change is always changing. The phrase "lasting change" is a contradiction in terms. There is no panacea. There is no ultimate, final change to end all change. There will always be the possibility for getting better. Thus, there will always be more changes to make. That's why schools will always need leaders, not just make-do managers.

Unlike some fields, changes in education are periodically recycled and reappear in a cyclical pattern. What goes around comes around. The same changes, in a repackaged format, keep popping up. Hopefully, they are refined and improved each time around.

There can be no growth without change (whether people want it or not). Change happens with or without design. There's no question that there will always be change, because it's the only way to improve. The only questions, if you want to be a leader, are what to change and when and how to do it.

DON'T CONFUSE COSMETIC CHANGES WITH REAL REFORM

While change, reform, and school improvement are the currencies of effective leadership, cosmetic or superficial changes can bankrupt a principal's or superintendent's credibility. Tinkering, tweaking, fine-tuning, employing smoke and mirrors, or merely rearranging the deck chairs should never be mistaken for or touted as real change.

Unfortunately, some school leaders delude or mislead their constituents (and, sometimes, themselves) into thinking that they are making substantive and significant changes, when, in reality, they are merely painting over real problems and diverting attention and effort from real solutions.

Managing change is hard work—too hard for some administrators. It's much easier to create the illusion of changing things than to go through all the effort to actually make real improvement. Below are the two most common ways that lazy, naïve, or misguided administrators give school reform a bad name:

1. *Renaming existing practices.* Change the name, but do the same. It's a common exercise. For example, some schools boast about providing students with "self-directed study time." Their parents simply called it "study hall." Some teachers now give students "enrichment activities." When you were a student, they called it "extra credit." Today's "acceleration" was yesterday's "skipping a grade." "Tracking" by any other name is still "ability grouping."

Attaching cute slogans, clever acronyms, popular buzz words, flashy phrases, or catchy labels to current programs is easy; but it is not meaningful reform. Good leaders don't confuse the language of change with the real thing.

2. *Making cosmetic changes.* Some school officials and other reformers (including politicians) often make a lot of noise when introducing high-sounding modifications that don't really make any difference. Examples of faux changes include adding more tests and calling it educational reform; increasing a program's budget, but not changing the program; and revising the symbols on the report card without altering standards or methods of evaluation.

Phony, superficial, or cosmetic changes seldom fool anyone—especially kids. ("Don't pee on my leg and tell me it's raining."—Judge Judy). But they can make a principal or superintendent look shallow, manipulative, or disingenuous. These are not the traits of an effective leader.

Real leaders make real changes. Language gimmicks, shell games, and bait-and-switch tricks don't count. If you want to be known as a change agent, do it right and do it at the right time.

WHEN TO CHANGE AND WHEN TO LEAVE WELL ENOUGH ALONE

If you take away only one thought after reading this leadership guide for school administrators, remember this: *Timing is everything!*

Ideas fail and leaders fall because of bad timing. When the timing is right, you can accomplish wonders; when the timing is wrong, forget it.

This is true for planning, for decision making, for getting the most out of people, and especially for implementing change.

The secret to achieving change is always in the timing. If you start at the wrong time, you may be destined for failure. If you wait too long, you may miss the window of opportunity. If you change too much too fast, you're likely to start losing people, and the entire organization can fall into disarray.

How, then, do leaders know when the time is right for change? It doesn't take a sixth sense. It just takes some common sense. (No leader should ever leave home without it.) Knowing when to move forward with change and when to hold back is the result of analyzing circumstances, assessing resources, weighing the odds, and balancing inertia against momentum. Sometimes, a little of that sixth sense called intuition actually does help as well.

If you're looking for guidelines, Table 4.1 can help you sort out when to change and when to leave well enough alone (no priorities are implied or intended).

When it's determined that the timing is right, effective leaders go all out in implementing desired change. (You can't just half change.) It sometimes helps maintain confidence to keep in mind that significant changes for the better almost always originate at the local level.

Because the best changes usually start closest to home, many of today's best school leaders choose to stay on the cutting edge at the building level rather than accept positions at the district, collegiate, state, or federal level. It's easier to change one building at a time, and you see results a lot sooner.

Once the ball starts rolling, the leader needs to be committed for the duration of the change process. It's easy to become impatient, but it won't help. Most well-planned and well-executed organizational changes follow a specific progression of sequential steps. Change occurs in phases. You can nudge things along, but normally you can't skip steps or rush the process very much.

UNDERSTANDING THE EVOLUTION OF A REVOLUTION: THE MANY FACES AND PHASES OF CHANGE

In Hollywood, most overnight successes have been 20 years in the making. Careers advance in stages. The same is true of school reform. Today's revolution usually had its roots in the past and has evolved through several separate phases over time.

Change just doesn't usually happen overnight. It tends to develop through a series of sequential steps. Changes in schools come about more like gradual global warming than as the result of a sudden thunderbolt. In schools, as in most organizations, the change process is more evolution than revolution.

Table 4.1   Guidelines for When to Change and When Not to Change

When to Change	When Not to Change
When things are going all wrong	When there aren't sufficient resources to pull it off
When things are going too right and complacency is breaking out all over	When it costs too much
	When literally no one else wants to do it
When kids are hurting	When the only reason to do it is the wrong reason (e.g., to make you look good or to benefit adults, not kids)
When your school is behind and has to catch up	
When parents and students ask for it	When emotions are running too high
When the school board demands it	When it might make things worse for kids
When the need is there and everyone knows it	When you don't have the right people to make it work
When the money's there	When you don't clearly understand the change
When your approval rate is high	
When new information, research, or insight shows clearly what needs to be done	When it doesn't make you excited or passionate
	When everyone is overloaded already
When it will make things better, easier, or more cost effective	When the staff is supersaturated with change or too burned out to take on any more for a while
When something new (e.g., legislation, a windfall) suddenly makes it possible	When it's time to sit back and solidify your gains
When just the right combination of people and resources falls into place	When it will prevent you from achieving more important goals
	When your boss says no
When your staff wants to "go for it"	When there are better choices
When you've always wanted to do it and you're tired of waiting	When the change is illegal, unethical, or unprofessional
When you know you can do this	When you're too new on the job
When it's now or never	When you're about to leave the job
When your gut says it's time	When it doesn't feel right

To make change happen, leaders need to understand the many faces and phases of change. With this understanding, leaders can measure progress, keep track of where they are in the process, and plot their next steps.

Different authorities break down the change process in different ways. Some say it has only two basic phases: start-up and follow-up. The noted researcher Kurt Lewin describes a three-step approach to implementing change:

1. *Unfreezing*—becoming open-minded

2. *Transition*—making a series of alterations

3. *Refreezing*—making the alterations routine

Other, more cynical observers liken the change process to the popular, tongue-in-cheek definition of team building: forming, storming, norming, and performing.

All of these oversimplifications may capture the essence of the process, but they're not much help with understanding the nitty-gritty of changing a complex human organization.

There is always value in keeping the change process as simple and uncomplicated as possible. Nevertheless, there are certain steps that normally have to be taken in order to alter organizational behavior dramatically.

If you want to bring about change, as most leaders do, please refer to the stages listed below through which you need to pass. These stages may be abbreviated or telescoped. Sometimes, they are handled quickly and informally, but they are seldom ignored completely.

The steps below constitute a generic model for effecting organizational change. Any leader can use them—they apply equally well to businesses, service agencies, nonprofit organizations, and schools.

Models are always helpful, but they are a lot more beneficial when accompanied by a user's manual. That's what the next section provides.

CHANGE STRATEGIES THAT REALLY WORK IN TODAY'S SCHOOL CLIMATE

Sometimes, school officials know the theory of change and understand the classic model (the process) for change, but it still never happens in their school or school system. Why? Because no one has ever helped them translate theory into action by spelling out the specifics of how to get started and how to follow through.

That's about to change. Following are 10 user-friendly tips and strategies for implementing real-world changes in your school starting today.

1. Accept the risk. Realize that every change comes with a cost. When things are changed, something is always lost or traded off. Be sure change is worth it before you start.

2. Concentrate on no more than two changes at a time. Any more blurs focus and diffuses energies.

3. Be careful how you phrase your goals and plans. Words are powerful. They shape how people will think and feel about proposed change. Picking the right metaphor can help push your plan over the top.

4. Prepare a timetable and stick to it. Most changes shouldn't take longer than 12 months from start to finish, because it's hard to maintain concentration and sustain maximum effort much longer than that. Allow enough time for each step in the process, but keep pressing fiercely forward.

5. Let everyone in who wants in. Give everyone a job. The intellectuals on the staff can help with planning and developing a well-thought-out rationale. The computer hackers can simulate alternative scenarios and provide technical support. The doers can see that things keep moving along on schedule. If everyone has a part to play, he or she will feel more ownership and exhibit more enthusiasm.

6. Deal with critics early. If you don't, they can sabotage your efforts at any step along the way.

7. Don't be overly incremental. Take big steps when you can. Move change along as quickly as you can without skipping essential steps. If the process drags on too long, people lose interest.

8. Use cheerleading to turn inertia into momentum. Publicize successes throughout the process. Give credit and recognition to everyone who contributes.

9. Constantly measure and reward the behavior you want.

10. Have a back-up plan in case the project crashes.

No matter how many proved strategies (such as those above) you follow, each change process is unique. There will always be surprises, disappointments, and miracles along the way. Be ready for them.

Stages in the Change Process

(Note the similarities between this process and the strategic planning process outlined in Chapter 2. Planning is the way effective leaders change things.)

I. Recognition Stage

(This is the awareness phase.)
- Identify and define the need.
- Own the problem.
- Adopt a "We've got to do something" attitude.

II. Exploration Stage

(This is the muddling phase.)
- See what's out there (explore the options).
- Brainstorm possibilities.
- Do the homework.
- Ask "What if?" questions.
- Allow an incubation period.

III. Lock-In Stage
- Zero in on the preferred remedy.
- Articulate the desired change.
- Develop a rationale.
- Give the project a name. (A catchy title can give the project a boost. Acronyms are always popular.)

Stages in the Change Process

IV. Planning Stage
- Chart the course.
- Set short- and long-term goals.
- Define the risks.
- Identify your allies and opponents.
- Establish a timetable.
- Identify the obstacles and strategies to overcome them.
- Assign responsibilities.
- Set up a budget.
- Establish benchmarks.

V. Readiness Stage
- Lay the foundation and set the stage.
- Overcome apathy.
- Marshal resources.
- Get staff on board.
- Gain support. (Line up all the help you can get.)
- Answer all questions.

VI. Implementation Stage
- Start the ball rolling.
- Announce the plan (once it's public).
- Do the paperwork.
- Work the plan.

VII. Evaluation Stage
- Monitor progress.
- Gather and document data.
- Take samples.
- Measure results against expectations.
- Get outside assessments if necessary.

VIII. Fine-Tuning Stage
- Refine procedures.
- Make midcourse corrections.
- Adjust the project as needed.
- Weed out what's not working.
- Renew effort.

IX. Routinization Stage
- Celebrate arrival at your destination.
- Make the new way of doing things the way you do business now.
- Put it in the handbook.
- Make it part of the everyday vocabulary.
- Make it part of the training for newcomers.
- Keep at it until it feels normal.

X. Up-Periscope Stage
- Take your time. Up the periscope only when you're ready.
- Scan the horizon.
- Look at what else needs to be done.
- Repeat the process.

Quick and Easy Time Allotment for a 1-Year Change Process

Gathering (collecting information)	2 months
Hunting (seeking solutions)	2 months
Planting (doing readiness activities)	2 months
Cultivating (nurturing change to fruition)	6 months
Harvesting (reaping rewards)	Indefinite

HOW TO SELL NEW IDEAS AND MAKE THEM WORK

Most school administrators-managers work pretty evenly. They handle everything in about the same way, with the same degree of intensity and energy. Effective leaders, however, realize that some things warrant extra effort. That's why they pay special attention to good beginnings and good endings. This is particularly true in orchestrating change.

When leaders in any field initiate change, they realize that it requires constant attention throughout the entire process. It's never over until it's over. The most important part is every part. Nevertheless, good beginnings and good endings are always special.

Getting the change process off to a solid beginning means successfully selling the new idea to the necessary stakeholders. If this doesn't happen, the proposed change isn't going anywhere.

At the other end of the continuum, ensuring a good ending means seeing to it that the new idea continues to have life after the change process is concluded. Sometimes, a carefully planned and executed change process is completed, people feel good about it, and then the new idea goes on the shelf; a year later, there's no trace of the innovation in the day-to-day operation of the organization.

When leaders want to tip the scale in favor of any particular change, they concentrate more on the kick-off and the follow-up.

From a good beginning to a good ending, change is the lifeblood of all vibrant organizations. Whether it's in a school or a factory, change obviously doesn't happen without a good deal of help from a knowledgeable leader. Below are suggestions to help you succeed in bringing new ideas to your school.

Fifteen Tips for Successfully Selling a New Idea

1. Sell the idea both up and down the line. You need support from the top to the bottom of the organization.

2. Use statistics and other data to get your point across, but avoid overkill. If your listener's eyes begin to glaze over, you've gone too far.

3. Remember that people will accept your idea more readily if they like you. That's why it's always wise to work on relationships.

4. Use persuasive power words and phrases, such as
   - user-friendly
   - state-of-the-art
   - innovative
   - cost effective
   - breakthrough
   - cutting edge

5. Model the desired type of changed behavior.

6. Give pep talks when necessary.

7. Don't oversell. Know when to shut up. Don't anesthetize your audience. You want them receptive, not comatose.

8. Don't apologize about costs.

9. Emphasize benefits. Whenever possible, show the payoffs for students, staff, and the community.

10. Anticipate and address possible risks, negative consequences, and adverse outcomes. Be realistic.

11. Let your passion show. Passion, enthusiasm, and commitment are powerful and persuasive.

12. Appeal to pride, lofty goals, and basic instincts and make use of authority, expert opinion, historical precedent, or whatever works to sell your idea.

13. Be sensitive to timing.

14. Plan to sell parents twice—once when they hear about the new idea at school, and again after they get home and think about it.

15. Use plain talk. Jargon doesn't sell ideas to laypeople and nonprofessionals.

Ten Tips for Making New Ideas Work

1. Hold periodic reunions of all those who contributed to the change.

2. Ask for regular "How's it going?" reports.

3. Make the changed behavior part of the performance appraisal system.

4. Conduct follow-up studies to see if the new idea is still working.

5. Channel budget support toward perpetuating the change.

6. Reward advocates who helped implement the change by giving them new responsibilities.

7. Keep the change alive through annual reports, parent newsletters, and other publications.

8. Use the changed behavior as part of the criteria for approval of future change proposals.

9. Keep demonstrating support from the top.

10. Brag about the change. Doing so helps make the change part of the culture of the organization.

As a school administrator, if you're not changing things, you're merely "doing" things. That's what old-style managers do best. But effective leaders don't like just "doing things." That's what makes them leaders.

Doing things or changing things? Managing the organization or leading it? When you're a principal or superintendent, it's your choice. Which will it be?

5

Spending Time

Being a principal, superintendent, or any other school administrator (even a mediocre one) is a full-time job. Providing life-changing leadership takes even more time. How do leaders do it?

One of the most observable differences between true leaders and also-rans in any organization is how they spend their time. Leaders don't do more things than other hardworking folks. They just do different things. It's true in all fields.

Leaders don't have more time than anyone else. They just make better use of their time on and off the job. Time management is simply making choices. Better choices mean better time use. Effective school leaders make the right choices more often than most people do. It starts by determining who's boss when it comes to time.

WHO CONTROLS A LEADER'S TIME?

If other people control how you use your time, who's leading whom? How many superintendents and principals do you know who show up every morning to find what's been planned for them? How many of these would you call real leaders? Effective leaders take a firmer stand on time.

Proactive leaders put themselves in charge of their own time by choosing to use it to their best advantage. They don't let too many other people mess with their calendar. If you ask successful leaders, they can predict with a high degree of accuracy what they will be doing a week from today. Many managers aren't sure what they'll be doing after lunch.

Men and women who lead and succeed do a better job at getting a full 60 seconds out of every minute than do most people because they understand the psychology of time. If you want to become more of a leader and less of a manager, you may have to change the way you think about time. If you alter your frame of reference, you can start seeing it the way most leaders do.

Time isn't the enemy. It's not an obstacle or an unfair restraint. Time is a working condition, it's a tool. Time is a resource much like money—but not entirely like money. Time can be counted, budgeted, spent, and even squandered, but it can't be invested to earn interest. Time can't grow. It can only shrink.

Most muddling managers fuss and fume about not having enough time. They blame time (or lack of it) for their shortcomings. They're wrong. It's not time's fault.

The way to begin gaining more control over time is to take stock of how you spend your daily and weekly allowance now. Most administrators don't actually use their time the way they think they do. Find out how you spend yours by keeping a daily log of activities for a week or two and then evaluating your time use. Be a harsh critic of how you spend your time. It helps to ask the questions listed in the below Personal Time Use Inventory.

Once you've identified how you really spend your days, weigh that information against what you should be doing in order to provide more and better leadership. You don't want to become a time management maniac, but you do want to control your time more than it controls you. Good leaders plan every day, not just the busiest days. Planning starts by establishing criteria for where you want to expend your energies. What's the best use of your time?

Personal Time Use Inventory

- What routine jobs, meetings, and other functions take up the most time?
- What am I doing that I shouldn't be doing?
- What jobs could be done better in another way or by someone else?
- How do I waste time each day?
- Who are the important people with whom I don't spend enough time?
- What tasks take up more time than they are worth?
- What do I do that is just plain dumb?
- What do I do regularly that makes me angry or frustrated?
- Do I have a reason for what I do?
- What time uses do I complain about to others the most?
- What jobs make me depressed?
- What jobs make me feel good?

SETTING PRIORITIES: PAPER VERSUS PEOPLE

It shouldn't come as a news flash that top-notch leaders in all fields spend more of their time with people than with paper. It's not by chance, it's by choice. That's part of what makes them leaders.

Some administrators prefer paperwork. It's safe, and it's quiet. Paper doesn't talk back. Paperwork is measurable. You know when you're done. You can see the results. It's OK to like shuffling papers. It's a legitimate function—but it's not leadership. I've never met a leader who liked paperwork.

Effective leaders direct their energies toward people because that's where their energy comes from. People are where the good ideas are. People create the problems and the solutions. People spawn action. People do the dreaming and make the dreams come true. People do the work.

Leaders lead people, whereas managers leave a paper trail. When it comes to deciding how to spend time, leaders choose peoplework over paperwork whenever they can (see Table 5.1).

Many average school administrators are always busy with paper and never seem to have enough time for people. Really good leaders know the difference between busyness and productivity and have enough time for everyone.

If you want to make the leap from management to leadership, a good first step is to spend more time with students, staff, parents, school board members, politicians, community leaders, taxpayers, senior citizens, business

Table 5.1   How Managers and Leaders Spend Their Time

Leaders Prefer Peoplework	Managers Prefer Paperwork
Informing	Researching
Instructing	Documenting
Inspiring	Outlining
Meeting	Drafting
Mentoring	Writing
Motivating	Rewriting
Conferencing	Proofreading
Coaching	Correcting
Coaxing	Record keeping
Teaching	Filling out forms
Persuading	Making applications
Influencing	Sorting paper
Negotiating	Processing paper
Lobbying	Organizing paper
Listening	Filing paper
Observing	Corresponding
Presenting	Studying
Schmoozing	Reading about work

representatives, ordinary citizens, and anyone else who can help or be helped by the school.

Get out of the office and into the school and the community. Seek out winners. Build bridges. Open up channels of communication. Share information. Listen and learn. Network. Make new contacts. Form partnerships. Forge coalitions. Work on relationships. These are the things the best leaders do.

How a leader spends time sends a message about what's important in the organization. When "peoplework" takes precedence over paperwork, the message is "people are most important." If school administrators don't send this message, who will?

HOW EFFECTIVE SCHOOL LEADERS SPEND 1,440 MINUTES PER DAY

Time is a constant resource. You can't add to it or multiply it, but the time you have belongs to you (unless you give it away or let someone else take it away from you). Part of the success and survival of leaders today depends on their gaining maximum control of that time.

The people we think of as leaders seem to get more done in the same amount of time than others do. They don't let time push them around. What do they do differently? Almost everything.

Below are a dozen of the most powerful and popular time stretchers that work well for leading principals and superintendents everywhere. Try them. They may change the way you work forever.

1. Delegate more than most administrators do. It's the chief way to get more out of people.

2. Stay focused on your priorities. It's easy to set them aside and forget them. Don't.

3. Always follow up and follow through. Make it your trademark. This is where many would-be leaders fall short. Even a great idea that is brilliantly conceived and launched with enormous fanfare ends up nowhere without proper follow-up and follow-through. Hoopla without payoff is wasted time.

4. Make the best use of your "prime time." Use your biological clock to your advantage. If you're a morning person, do the hard stuff and schedule the most important meetings before noon.

5. Plan to be spontaneous.

6. Know your weak spots. (Be strong enough to admit weakness.) Let someone better tackle tasks in these areas.

7. Pace yourself. Work as fast as you can but as slow as you need to.

8. Mentally rehearse events in advance. It helps to have a mental map of each upcoming day.

9. Be better organized than you appear to be.

10. Tackle problems sooner rather than later.

11. Don't give every task the same effort; just give every task the effort it deserves.

12. Spend time planning how to spend time.

These techniques can help you squeeze every ounce of productivity out of every hour of the day. They work for many leaders in all fields. They're free. They're available for anyone to use.

Obviously, stand-out leaders approach time differently, think about it differently, and use it differently. If you want to act like a leader and be perceived as a leader, start using your time the way leaders do. Here's how successful leaders typically spend their 1,440 minutes per day:

- Leaders spend a lot of time each day performing the three classic leadership functions (planning, directing, and controlling) with a modern twist. In today's leadership terms, this means visioning, goal setting, motivating, training, setting standards, measuring, evaluating, and ensuring quality control. If you're not involved in these kinds of activities on a daily basis, you're not on a projectory toward leadership.
- Leaders spend the bulk of their day every day working on things that are most important to their job and that can't be done by someone else. All other tasks can be left to others.
- Leaders try to spend as much time as possible every day doing what they do best. All leaders possess certain skills or talents (star qualities) that caused them to stand apart from others in the organization. These shouldn't be hidden or wasted just because the person has been propelled into a leadership position. To the extent possible, leaders keep on doing what has always worked for them in the past.
- Leaders have to spend some time daily in handling routine matters (e.g., processing mail, returning calls, etc.). These are necessary activities. No phone calls or e-mail, voice mail, or regular mail messages should go unanswered for more than 24 hours. Nevertheless, routine should be contained within a small fraction of each day. It should never make up the whole day.
- Leaders spend some time almost daily giving back to their community. It's not in the job description, but it's part of a true leader's life. Many managers like to think they don't have time for community service. Leaders know they have to make time for it.

- Leaders devote time every day to tipping the scale toward a more balanced life. This means taking care of themselves (exercising, resting properly, eating right); nurturing friendships; spending time with family members; nourishing the spirit; and having fun. If you can't find or make time for these activities, you're not the leader of the organization. You're a slave to it.
- Leaders set aside a portion of each day (even if it's only a matter of minutes) for quiet time devoted to prayer, meditation, imaging, or just daydreaming. Quietude is an elixir that every leader needs.

These are the activities that make up a genuine leader's day. How does it compare to your day?

To be able to use time doing the right things, leaders have to avoid spending time doing the wrong things. This means watching out for certain common time-use traps.

THE TEN WORST TIME-USE MISTAKES

Everyone makes mistakes—even leaders. Some mistakes cost money. Some cost time. The latter may be the most costly in the long run.

Peak performance requires economical and efficient time use. This means relentlessly sticking to targeted tasks and skirting time traps that con many people into unproductive and counterproductive behavior. Fortunately, good leaders don't con easily.

Real leaders don't make many time-use mistakes. Would-be and wannabe leaders make many without even realizing it. Every misspent minute may be a missed opportunity for making a difference. That's why successful leaders do their best to stay away from the most common time wasters and time traps. The difference between winners and losers isn't just in how they spend their time but in how they don't spend it as well.

School administrators don't make more time-use mistakes than managers in other professions, but they often make different ones. The inclusive culture of the school serves as an enabler for certain kinds of inefficiencies. Besides the common time wasters already spelled out in Chapter 3 are the "Top 10 Time-Use Mistakes" listed above and explored in more detail below. These are some of the most frequent offenses that rob well-meaning administrators of what they need most to become leaders—time.

Solving other people's problems. It's common for employees to buck problems up the ladder. It's also common for administrators up the line to let them. Administrators like to help and to show off their problem-solving abilities. That's why they often willingly take on others' problems. It's a mistake. The old saying "Just because someone throws you a ball doesn't mean you have to catch it" applies. Time spent on others' problems is time not spent on leadership functions. Leaders support and empower employees to solve their own problems. They don't solve the problems for them.

Top Ten Time-Use Mistakes

1. Solving other people's problems

2. Oversupervising

3. Excessive socializing

4. Doing the wrong job

5. Acting without thinking

6. Forming too many committees

7. Putting undue effort into low-yield projects

8. Reading the wrong stuff

9. Walking on eggs

10. Serving the wrong master or masters

Oversupervising. Micromanagement should be a felony. It stifles initiative and creativity throughout the organization. Unfortunately, many school boards, superintendents, principals, and other school administrators are guilty of oversupervising. A lackluster organization is their punishment. Micromanagement isn't just a neutral use of time, it's a negative use. Effective leaders breathe life into the organization without breathing over everyone's shoulders.

Excessive socializing. Camaraderie is a sign of a healthy organization. However, too much water cooler gossip, teacher's lounge small talk, and idle chitchat add up to too much time off task. Leaders are supposed to spend lots of time with people and have fun in the process. This doesn't mean that socializing should replace supervision. The rule that many leaders follow is simply: be accessible, be friendly, be businesslike, and be the boss when you have to.

Doing the wrong job. Some aspiring leaders do a good job of doing the wrong job. Often, they revert back to their old job because it feels comfortable, or they borrow parts of someone else's job because it looks easier or more fun than their own. It's easy to do the wrong job when the right job is a lot harder. Nevertheless, leaders aren't supposed to do just whatever looks good to them or whatever they want to do. Leaders are supposed to do what leaders do. Anything else is a misuse of their time.

Acting without thinking. Rash acts result in a disproportionate number of mistakes or blunders that have to be undone or redone. Correcting mistakes and practicing damage control are preventable exercises. The time could be better spent in more positive and proactive activities. Leadership is both thinking and doing. The thinking part comes first.

Forming too many committees. School personnel are notorious for setting up task forces and study groups. Wherever a new problem or issue arises, many educators automatically throw a committee at it. Some large school districts even have a committee on committees to keep track of all of its other committees. Committees never speed things up and often bog everything down. Most committees have only three speeds: slow, slower, and stop. Too often, they use up valuable time and other resources while producing few results. As one committee-weary administrator observed, "Not all committees are bad. Some are harmless." It's not surprising that most leaders prefer direct action to committee work whenever possible.

Putting undue effort into low-yield projects. Some pseudoleaders do an incredible job of moving molehills. They put in lots of time working on tasks or projects that don't amount to much. It's called overkill, and it's a waste of time. Real leaders save their major efforts for major undertakings.

Reading the wrong stuff. All educators are deluged with reports, studies, letters, memos, faxes, e-mail messages, articles, books, advertisements, and other junk mail. Because they're in the business of teaching reading, it's natural for school administrators to feel compulsive about reading everything that comes to their attention. It's a time trap. Much of what crosses their desks doesn't deserve to be read or can better be read off duty. It's a mistake to use too much time reading on the job. Time-conscious leaders read the right stuff at the right time and leave the junk mail to others.

Walking on eggs. Some administrators are too nice to be leaders. They don't want to hurt anyone's feelings, so they beat around the bush, give out mixed messages, issue veiled warnings, and drop hints rather than offer honest criticism or deliver direct reprimands or ultimatums. You can't lead by innuendo. Straight talk works. Pussyfooting around tough topics doesn't. Effective leaders say what has to be said and move on. It reduces confusion, minimizes misunderstandings, and saves time for more productive leadership tasks.

Serving the wrong master or masters. Arguably, school administrators have too many bosses. They can't all be served equally. It's not uncommon for administrators to make the mistake of serving the wrong one. We all know school officials who truly believe that their job is to make their boss or the school board "look good." (An impossible challenge in many situations.) These administrators are spending their time serving the wrong master. There's a difference between a lackey and a leader. The administrators who really make a difference as leaders are the ones who spend their time making kids look good, not other adults.

All of the time traps above can be avoided. The best defense against making stupid time-use mistakes is simply to say "no" more often. "No" is a tool. Insecure managers hesitate to use it. Confident leaders use it a lot.

WHEN AND HOW TO SAY NO

Saying no isn't always a negative response. It can be just another way of setting priorities. Sometimes, saying no is the most positive response a leader can make. It's often the easiest, quickest, and cleanest way to clear your calendar of nuisance duties and needless projects in order to make way for the real work of leadership. They don't teach that in graduate school.

Knowing when to say no is an important survival skill for anyone who heads up any kind of organization today. Leaders understand and respect the power of *no*. It is a valuable help in preserving perspective and avoiding involvement in things that don't merit their attention. If you can't say no, you may not be decisive enough to make tough leadership choices for your department, school, or school system.

There are many times when no is the only right answer. Below are everyday examples of common situations where it's prudent and productive to turn down a request, opportunity, invitation, new project, or added duty. Effective leaders just say no when the following occur:

- They have too many irons in the fire already. It's either deception or denial to keep adding more activities to an overloaded schedule. Leaders gain more respect by saying no than by letting down everyone (including themselves) because they took on too much.
- They really hate the idea or activity. When people, even those who are in charge, take on tasks they despise, they usually do a poor job and feel lousy in the process.
- The idea is an obvious loser. If a project is stupid and unworkable, no leader wants to get involved. Someone should have said no to the Edsel project when it first came up in the Ford Motor Company.
- The project or proposal doesn't elicit any passion or excitement. Lack of enthusiasm almost always leads to a lackluster performance.
- There's nothing to learn or no growth potential. Leaders try to accept only new challenges that promise to make them better leaders or better human beings.
- It's the right project but the wrong time. (Remember, timing is everything.) If a project is an idea whose time has not yet come, effective leaders wait until the time is right.
- It's not worth the effort. Careers aren't built tackling time wasters.
- It's phony. Made-up projects serve no legitimate purpose.
- There's a better way to do it. It's foolish to waste time and effort on second-best projects.
- It doesn't feel right. Intuition works.

Of course, knowing how to say no is as important as knowing when to say it. There's no use saying it if you don't mean it or can't make it stick. Many leaders say that the right way to turn down requests is to follow three simple rules of refusal:

1. Be firm and clear in declining the opportunity.

2. Give a reason for your response.

3. Be willing to repeat your response as often as it takes.

When it's the right choice, saying no feels good. It works. It gets easier with practice. Saying no is a time-saving, work-smarter technique. It's a necessary part of every successful leader's vocabulary.

OTHER WORK-SMARTER WAYS TO SAVE TIME

Leadership takes time. Leaders have the time because they know how to cut corners, combine tasks, streamline procedures, sidestep time traps, and work smarter than most people. They're not born with this knowledge. They learn it. You can too. Below are some more work-smarter strategies and techniques that anyone can use.

- Hoard ideas. Be shameless about picking other people's brains. Keep your antenna up for new approaches or solutions wherever you may find them. Store them for future reference. You can never have too many good ideas on hand.
- Don't underestimate the power of lists. Making lists is another form of planning. Good leaders make them and follow them every day.
- Have a plan for handling interruptions.
- Use your wastebasket more than your filing cabinet.
- Avoid giving incomplete or fuzzy instructions. They always have to be repeated.
- Watch what you eat during the workday. It can affect performance for several hours after a meal. For maximum mental alertness, limit your caloric intake. Also keep in mind that a healthy snack can help you bounce back when lethargy sets in and impairs the ability to get things done.
- Practice "calendar integrity." Keep your appointments and commitments. Be on time. If you don't waste others' time, they won't waste yours.
- Set aside blocks of time in which to batch similar tasks.
- Never hesitate to ask for help as soon as you need it. It's a sign of maturity and professionalism, not weakness.
- Build in interruption time. Make allowance for something unexpected to happen, because it always does.
- Remember the 3 Ds of handling junk mail:
  1. Don't request it.
  2. Don't accept it.
  3. Don't read it.

- Don't spend time posturing. Peacocks are beautiful, but you don't see many other birds following their lead.
- Remember that much of what schools do floats on a stream of paper. Schools use forms for everything. Streamline your organization's forms. Make them easier to differentiate, read, fill out, and process. You'll save time for yourself and others.
- Don't get too enamored with executive perks. A cushy office and too many other creature comforts can distract from hard work.
- Practice "benign neglect" by ignoring minor crises and issues that will probably resolve themselves, be resolved by others, or go away with the passage of time.

Whereas many managers run out of time, real leaders run *into* time by finding ways to do things better, quicker, more efficiently, or not at all, as in the examples above. "Found time" is the grist of leadership. Fortunately, there's no big secret about working smarter anymore.

So much has been written about time management that there isn't much new to say or learn about it. The key now is to do what we already know. It doesn't take any more knowledge to use time wisely—just more will. Leaders have it. Many also-ran managers don't. What about you?

6

Handling Politics

Educators aren't dumb, but lots of them are surprisingly ignorant when it comes to organizational politics. Many still think that schools are above petty politics. Likewise, some prospective school leaders really believe that they can get by without politics. Wrong on both counts.

POLITICS AND SCHOOLS

Politics is a fact of life in all organizations, and schools are no exception. In fact, because schools are full of people wielding power over other people, most school systems are permeated with politics.

This isn't necessarily a bad thing. Unfortunately, bad politicians have given politics a bad name. In essence, politics is neither good nor bad. It just is.

Wherever there is power to be had, resources to be divided, recognition to be earned, or influence to be brokered, there is politics. Wherever there are leaders and followers, there is politics. That's everywhere. If you think you can become an effective school leader without being involved in politics, you're kidding yourself. You're already involved whether you know it or not.

All effective school leaders are also political leaders. (The best ones are so skillful at it that they aren't readily recognized as being political.) It's really misleading even to say that school leaders "play" politics. It's not a game; the stakes are too important. Politics isn't play; it's hard work. Politics is another basic tool that all successful leaders use to achieve goals through other people.

Politics isn't some evil, dark discipline. It's just one more way to use relationships to get things done. Good leaders understand this and use politics to their advantage. This requires understanding power structures and learning when to negotiate and when to draw the line.

Schools are a particularly unique mix of internal and external political forces, including staff factions, student cliques, special interest groups (e.g., parents of gifted students or hockey boosters), district personnel, the school board, city lawmakers, state legislatures, and more. Principals and superintendents who want to lead must learn to read the political power swings within the organization and to activate, unite, and integrate diverse political forces behind common goals.

Fortunately, for most of us, political skills are honed, not inherited. You don't have to be a born glad-hander or backslapper to become politically effective. You just have to understand how the system works and how to work it.

The leaders who survive and succeed in the politically charged environment of today's schools align themselves with issues and ideas rather than with factions or personalities. Of equal importance, they steadfastly resist compromising principles for personal gain.

The best advice for all school officials is to take the high road in dealing with organizational politics. This means using "good" politics when necessary and avoiding "bad" politics altogether.

GOOD POLITICS, BAD POLITICS

The politics within any organization is only as good or as bad as the people in the organization make it. Unfortunately, some bad professional politicians have tainted the popular perception of all politics. Too often, politics is associated with graft and corruption. It doesn't have to be that way.

Politics can be as bad as collusion, malfeasance, and kickbacks or as good as listening to constituents and seeking the greatest good for the greatest number. Most organizations include both good and bad political practices and practitioners (see Table 6.1). If you think your school is different, look again.

Sometimes, overly ambitious administrators or misguided managers see questionable office politics as a shortcut to power within the organization. It doesn't work. Dirty politics and public service don't mix—ever! Particularly in the public sector and especially in schools, any glory, power, or recognition gained by cutthroat political maneuvering or manipulation is short lived. Real leaders want to leave a more lasting legacy.

If you want to develop into an effective educational leader, it's OK to be political, but it's never OK to

- Do anything illegal or unethical
- Violate professional ethics or school policy

Table 6.1   Examples of Political Practices of School Personnel

Good Politics	Bad Politics
Compromise	Dirty tricks
Consensus building	Exploiting weaknesses
Persuasion	Stonewalling
Open debate	Cronyism
Coalitions and alliances	Abuse of power
Lobbying	Pork barrel
Exchange of favors	Buying favors
Negotiating	Political blackmail
Practicality and pragmatism	Recrimination
Reality checks	Coercion and abusive control
Covering each other's back	Manipulation

- Constantly switch allegiance to whatever personality, faction, or position is popular at the moment
- Lie, cheat, or steal
- Take unfair advantage of others' weaknesses
- Spread false rumors
- Disrespect privacy or confidentiality
- Falsify records or test results
- Harass vulnerable parties
- Misuse authority

Political expediency may be slick, opportunistic management, but it's not leadership, and it's a far cry from statesmanship. Good leaders stick to good politics—period!

What works for most successful school leaders is to be political but to remain authentic and principled at the same time. After all, it's not just an adult's reputation at stake. There are children involved as well.

To establish the level of credibility needed to lead people, change organizations, and make things better, just being squeaky clean isn't good enough. It's not merely a cliché that public officials have to avoid even the perception of impropriety. It's reality.

As an example, the best principals and superintendents meticulously separate all partisan political involvement from any work-related activities. To help both teachers and administrators, some systems have adopted political activity guidelines similar to the ones shown below. If your school or district doesn't have such guidelines, it should.

Any of the tools of leadership can be misused. That doesn't make them bad tools. Just because communication can be misleading doesn't mean that leaders should quit communicating. Just because motivation can turn into manipulation doesn't mean that leaders should stop motivating. The same is true of politics.

Guidelines for Political Activity of School Personnel

1. The circulation of campaign literature for any candidate through school facilities is prohibited.

2. School personnel shall not participate in political activities during the regular duty day.

3. School personnel shall not solicit, enlist, or organize students for any political activity during the school day.

4. School equipment and supplies shall not be used in the preparation or distribution of political materials.

5. If candidates are invited to speak at the school, all major candidates for the same position should be invited.

If you want to move beyond being a cut-and-dried school administrator to become a cutting-edge leader, don't be afraid of politics. Just be careful how you use it so that you don't end up being used in the process.

HOW TO BE POLITICALLY SAVVY: "STREET SMARTS" FOR SCHOOL LEADERS

Survival-conscious principals and superintendents don't get caught up in playing petty political games, but they have to learn how to work with and around the internal and external politics of the situation.

To become a successful leader, every administrator needs to develop a degree of political savvy or "street smarts" for getting things done in the organization. Leaders don't engage in dirty politics (they don't have to)— but they know how to. Being street smart about politics in the school merely means understanding how things really work in the trenches.

To remain above political infighting is one thing. To be so naïve as to deny the existence of political posturing, maneuvering, and one-upmanship is another. No leader can afford the latter.

The secret of educational leaders who stick around is that they consistently place professionalism over political behavior. The best ways to remain professional while practicing savvy political leadership are to develop collaborations, form coalitions, build partnerships, influence decisions, look for win-win situations, take risks, and share power. These are the means for using political know-how to achieve preferred results without resorting to cheap tricks or underhanded tactics.

To make the most of the positive side of politics while avoiding being tainted by the more seamy side of political activity, there are certain realities that every leader has to know or find out.

For starters, savvy leaders don't make the mistake of thinking that there is only one political system at work within the organization. There are many, including the following:

- Individual and group political agendas
- Overall organizational politics
- Politics with your boss and the school board
- Politics with peers
- Politics with subordinates
- External political pressures

Working with one set of political relationships and ignoring the others can be a fatal faux pas.

With this in mind, effective leaders earn their degree in street smarts by finding out as much as possible about who has the power, how it is used, and how things really get decided and done in the organization. The district organization chart on the first page of the policy manual won't tell you. You have to dig out this kind of information on your own by seeking answers to the following questions:

1. Who are the policymakers and who are the real power brokers in the system? How did they attain these roles?

2. Who are your friends? Who are your enemies? Who wants your job? Is anyone out to get you?

3. What are your supervisor's and the school board's hot buttons and hidden agendas?

4. Who is successful in the system? Why?

5. Who are the political phonies in the organization?

6. Who has the real power, and where do they get their clout?

7. Who are potential backstabbers and/or the most likely to go over your head?

8. Whose views are most compatible with your own? Least compatible?

9. Who's telling the truth? Whose word can you count on?

10. What political factions exist? How do they work?

Knowing the answers to these questions helps position a leader to exercise political clout. (Knowledge is power.) Understanding the inner workings of the organization is what observers call street smarts. Sometimes, it's better than a high IQ. It's a leadership trait they usually don't mention in Administration 101.

Once leaders have a good feel for how the organization works, then and only then are they really ready to use organizational politics to their advantage.

EVERYDAY POLITICAL STRATEGIES FOR TODAY'S SCHOOL LEADERS

Dealing with the politics of any organization is always tricky business because it involves working with attitudes and opinions that can change overnight, loyalties that are frequently fickle, relationships that can go sour, deals that can blow up, and alliances that can fall apart without warning. (Politics not only makes a strange bedfellow, it keeps some people from sleeping altogether.)

Politics in schools can be particularly complex because of the multitude of diverse political agendas (e.g., the separate agendas of parents, students, teachers, administrators, and the school board) competing for attention and recognition. That's why all really good leaders proceed with caution, using all of the information about the organization that they can gather and paying attention to their best political instincts at the same time.

Politics isn't a science, but it does follow principles such as the following: When someone or something is pushed, something else has to give; for every political action, there is a political reaction; and when a rumor is in motion, it tends to stay in motion. Effective leaders know these basic principles just as scientists know the laws of physics.

Ignorance of the "laws of politics" can be costly. Many would-be leaders falter because they never quite figure out what's really going on in the organization and, consequently, make naïve political mistakes or politically incorrect decisions.

The best leaders understand, respect, and are sensitive to the power of politics and the principles on which it operates. They use time-tested tactics and techniques to make politics work in their favor. That's what makes them leaders. Of course, the same strategies are available to everyone.

If you want to be on top of and make the most of internal and external politics, do what the leaders do—follow the suggestions below. They've been tried. They've passed the test. They work. There's no extra charge. They just may be the best political advice you'll ever get.

• Learn negotiating skills. They are invaluable in day-to-day political encounters, just as they are in collective bargaining. Watch how professional negotiators work. They know how to combine emotion and rhetoric with logic and deal making to get results. Negotiating isn't a mysterious process. It's just another name for organized give-and-take. That's what organizational politics is all about. It's what good leaders do all the time.

How to Spot Political Phonies

The most dangerous and damaging political phonies

- Focus on appearances
- Steal others' plans and ideas
- Specialize in double-talk
- Limit their friendships to those who can help with career advancement
- Are never around in times of emergency or trouble
- Never run out of excuses or alibis
- Undercut others behind their back
- Trade on others' weaknesses and vulnerabilities
- Make false promises
- Put personal gain over organizational goals
- Deal in disloyalty
- Use sex for political advantage if they can
- Take undeserved credit
- Spread false rumors or gossip
- Attack other people's personalities and characters
- Set others up for failure
- Shirk blame
- Disregard confidentiality
- Lie about performance and distort successes
- Cheat when it serves their purpose
- Really believe that their ends justify any means
- Try to build their careers on "brownie points"

- Make at least one good enemy. Enemies keep you honest and give you candid feedback that friends won't. When your enemies are especially upset with you, you know you're probably doing something right.

- Learn how the people with power (e.g., the superintendent, the school board, the legislature, etc.) like to receive information. Give them the information you want them to have in the way they want to get it. It maximizes your chances of being heard.

- Do everything you can to make yourself indispensable. It helps you ride out political storms. You want to be perceived as a "comer," not a "goner."

- Resist the temptation to play dirty politics, cut corners, or sacrifice values.

- Distance yourself from political losers (individuals and causes).

- Adjust to your boss's style as much as you can without losing your identity or abandoning your goals.

- Don't gloat over temporary political victories, and don't repeat other people's bad news. It's bad form, and it's bad politics.

- Know when to walk away from a bad idea or cause. Back off when it becomes apparent that the political odds are against you. There's nothing more pathetic than a self-deluded administrator trying to rally support for a project that everyone else knows is a dead issue. (Timing is everything.) If the political climate isn't right today, it may become more favorable tomorrow. You may not know for a little while that you've made yourself ridiculous and become politically impotent because you were too stupid or too stubborn to let go of a loser.

- Make concessions when the results are worthwhile. Most good things in life are a trade-off.

- Let people become indebted to you so that you can call in your markers later on if you need to.

- Learn when to lay low. When the bad stuff hits the fan, it's never dispersed equally. Some get hit with more than others, and it sticks. There are times when it's best to be low key, stand on the sidelines, and stay out of the line of fire.

- Get an edge on adversaries by looking at them from different perspectives. Rename the opposition. When you think of opponents as misguided or troubled people, rather than as bad people, you can deal with them more effectively.

- Watch your backside. Exercise "enlightened paranoia" to avoid being blindsided.

- Avoid showdowns. There's always the chance you might lose.

- Beware of empty threats. They seldom work, and they make you look weak.

- Let people know where you stand on the issues. It's an obligation. If you don't, you're not leading anyone anywhere. You're just trying to stay out of trouble.

- When people show you who they are, believe them. Second chances are one thing, but third and fourth chances are risks you don't need to take.

• Try to keep internal politics from spilling over into the community. If something negative leaks out, don't engage in a political war of words in or with the media. You can't win a battle with someone who buys ink by the barrel.

• Always have an "exit card." Effective leaders make sure they have someplace to go and something to do if things don't work out. Holding an exit card makes you a braver, bolder leader. It makes it easier to be your best and do what's right. It's hard to take risks when you're paralyzed by concerns about possible adverse consequences.

The measures above are what keep many leaders from becoming political casualties and allow them to stick around long enough to see how things turn out. Such political finesse is never more important than when dealing with political leaders who know (or think they know) the ropes better than you do.

TIPS ON WORKING WITH POLITICAL LEADERS

To get the resources and results they want, successful school administrators have to deal with political leaders and figures of all kinds. It's easy to be ineffective if you don't understand how highly political people operate or how the "political mind" works. Sometimes, it requires special approaches and considerations. The tips below provide useful guides for working with elected officials and other political leaders.

1. Expect political leaders to have a hidden agenda. (Their agenda doesn't have to be your agenda.)

2. Understand that in politics, people don't always say what they mean, and things are not always what they seem to be.

3. Do your job right every day—no matter which way the political winds are blowing.

4. Don't tie your star to any political figure. Shine in your own right.

5. Always put loyalty to kids and the organization over politics.

6. Don't be dazzled by rhetoric.

7. Don't cut deals or make promises you can't keep.

8. Never agree to get what you want by taking unfair advantage.

9. Remember, political figures come and go. The kids show up every day.

10. Fight for principles, not for political gain.

11. Don't expect or seek undeserved favors.

12. If it helps kids, let political leaders take some credit for your results.

13. Compromise lots of things—but not your ethics or your dignity.

14. If a political leader makes an offer that sounds too good to be true—well, you know.

15. In dealing with political leaders, as in dealing with others, if it doesn't feel right, don't do it.

As indicated above, politics is largely common sense. Unfortunately, some school personnel shy away from leadership roles because they don't think they're political enough. They don't think of themselves as "politicians." They don't want to get caught up in petty or dirty politics. They don't feel that they are politically sophisticated enough to succeed. They're overreacting and holding back for the wrong reasons. All administrators can learn enough politics to get by without becoming corrupt or losing their souls.

Effective school leaders have to be politically aware and capable of functioning in a political system, but they don't have to be full-time, old-time politicians. There's a lot you can do and get done without "playing politics."

HOW TO GET NOTICED, GET AHEAD, AND GET THINGS DONE WITHOUT PLAYING POLITICS

Politics can help, but long-lasting school leaders don't base their careers or their vision for the school exclusively on political gamesmanship. Mediocre leaders often put too much stock in politics and not enough in other dimensions of leadership, including hard work.

School administrators can't become leaders and leaders can't succeed if they don't get noticed. School boards, like corporate boards, tend to reward, promote, and support those who attract attention to themselves. It may not be fair, but it's reality. It should be no surprise that it takes a lot more than politics for a leader to gain the right kind of recognition.

Leaders who receive positive attention and the advantages that come with it know how to make themselves stand out—without "apple polishing" or playing petty politics. They know how to get noticed. It's a set of skills that can be acquired.

You don't have to be bigger, smarter, better looking, or more political than others to get recognized, get ahead, get your ideas accepted, and achieve your leadership goals. You just have to know how to get noticed. You can learn how to do it. Following are several ways for getting the right people to notice you and your work without resorting to political trickery.

1. Be first. Be fast. Get tasks done earlier than expected and before most others do. If your projects and reports always come in on time along with everyone else's, they may get lost in the shuffle. If your work gets done first, however, it's bound to be noticed. Principals and superintendents who consistently beat deadlines stand out. It's not politics. It's just intelligent leadership.

2. Be willing. Be receptive to added responsibilities. Working beyond the job description is a surefire way to stand out. Exceeding expectations is always a dramatic attention getter. All really good leaders do it. Administrators who go the extra mile distance themselves from the rest of the pack. It's hard to be inconspicuous when you're out in front.

If you gain a reputation as a leader who will do whatever it takes for as long as it takes, you won't need politics to get the recognition and the extra resources you need.

3. Be principled. Keep your word. Do the right thing—every time. Sooner or later, a reputation for integrity gets rewarded. Leaders who refuse to compromise their principles draw attention to themselves. Ethical and moral behavior never goes out of style, but it is rare enough today to get noticed. It's better than politics.

4. Be upbeat. In school systems, people at all levels shy away from naysayers and whiners. Instead, they rally around a leader who maintains a positive attitude about the job and the future. Stay positive and you'll get everyone's attention—including the school board's. It's hard to ignore buoyancy.

5. Be assertive. Overcome timidity. Express your views. Stand up for what you believe and speak out for what you think is right. Don't back down at the first sign of resistance or opposition. It may not be political, but it works. Being assertive isn't being argumentative, stubborn, or disagreeable. It's just being confident enough in your own judgment and opinions to defend your position and to actively "sell" your point of view. Confidence gets noticed. Most organizations value leaders who dare to take a stand.

6. Be yourself. Authenticity is a rare commodity today. That's why being yourself is one of the surest and swiftest ways to get noticed. In some school systems, principals and other leaders all strive to become carbon copies of the superintendent. That's why it's easy for a real person to stand out.

7. Refuse to be phony. You'll feel better about yourself while earning the respect of others. More importantly, you will be readily noticeable, and

you will get the positive attention you need to succeed without resorting to questionable political activity.

Good leaders realize that it pays to get noticed, but getting noticed doesn't happen by accident. Politics can help, but it's up to each leader to find other ways to get his or her share of the recognition needed to make things happen.

The bottom line is that lasting leaders have to use politics *and* all of the other tools of leadership described throughout this book in order to get noticed, get ahead, and get things done. If you're not willing to make the effort, you're reconciling yourself to remaining at a makeshift management level swallowing and following like most others in the organization. It may be settling for less than your best and less than you deserve.

7

Dealing With Setbacks

L eadership isn't just a series of successes. If it were, a lot more people would sign up. Unfortunately, even great leaders make mistakes, encounter failures, make poor judgment calls, run into unforeseen obstacles, or come face to face with Murphy's Law (anything that can go wrong, will). It's what happens next that marks a genuine leader. Circumstances don't create leaders, they reveal them.

SETBACKS HAPPEN

Somebody screws up. Computer systems crash. A bond issue fails. Test scores plummet. Budgets are cut. Plans backfire. Deals fall through. Setbacks happen. That's why schools need leaders.

Every school and school system experiences its share of goof-ups and disappointments. They happen to everyone. Some organizations, however, can bounce back from setbacks or crises and be better off for the experience. Others can't. The difference lies with the leader.

When things are OK, any leader will do. It's when things start to unravel that the organization finds out if it has a real leader or a lightweight at the helm.

Avoiding setbacks isn't the measure of an effective leader. That's an unrealistic expectation. It's how they respond to setbacks that sets superior leaders apart. When things go wrong, principals and superintendents can make the most of a bad situation or make matters worse.

In tough times, some administrators merely sulk and lick their wounds. Others pick up the pieces and press fiercely forward. Guess who the real leaders are? If you want to stick around very long as a leader, it pays to know what to do and what not to do when setbacks occur.

Of course, the best thing to do about setbacks is to prevent them in the first place. A good offense is still the best defense.

Most seasoned observers agree that school administrators, like managers in all fields, are often their own worst enemies when it comes to causing setbacks. Many reversals stem from the classic "six deadly sins" of management: pride, sloth (laziness), envy, greed, anger, and pessimism. (Sometimes, the seventh sin—bad luck—also plays a role.) Anything you can do to squelch these self-destructive forces will keep many setbacks from happening. Maturity, good judgment, grown-up behavior, and common sense are the best forms of setback insurance.

If the leader of the organization doesn't bring on self-inflicted problems, the people around the leader may. Many setbacks are the result of other people letting the leader down or betraying the leader's confidence in them. That's why it's always wise to hire loyal staff members who are smarter and better than yourself.

Other ways skillful leaders head off setbacks include

- Analyzing past errors to make sure they don't happen again

- Always giving clear directions and instructions (twice)

- Never assuming anything—checking things out

- Never giving things time to go wrong—starting quality control immediately

- Anticipating all the things that could go wrong and installing safeguards

- Always knowing something can go radically wrong—and never getting caught unprepared

Despite these measures, which are second nature to most leaders, miscues and setbacks still happen. When they do, an ordinary administrator might head for cover. Effective leaders come out swinging. They realize that no setback is the end of the world. ("A setback only paves the way for a comeback."—Evander Holyfield).

A setback is just a special kind of problem. It should be handled like any other problem. Look for causes, correct them, consider options, pick one, and go for it.

Handling reversals is a test. If you pass, you're well on your way to becoming a successful leader. Fortunately, help is available. There are many effective ways to stave off setbacks and to deal with them when they occur. You should know, however, that worry isn't one of them.

WORRYING ONLY MAKES IT WORSE

If you're a worrier, maybe you shouldn't be a leader. Leaders have a lot to worry about. Fortunately, most don't. They understand what worry does and doesn't do (See Table 7.1), and they don't want anything to do with it.

Table 7.1   Why Worry?

What Worrying Does	What Worrying Doesn't Do
Wastes time	Solve anything
Creates stress	Teach you anything
Saps energy	Make problems go away
Encourages insomnia	Prevent setbacks
Speeds aging	Make you feel better
Causes wrinkles	Boost confidence
Brings on health problems	Enhance your image
Affects others	Equip you to better solve future problems

All worrying is destructive and infectious. It can't keep setbacks from happening, and it can't help overcome them when they pop up. It's not just nonproductive behavior, it's counterproductive. There is absolutely nothing beneficial about worrying.

That's why successful leaders spend less time worrying than other people and use the time saved to do something more positive, constructive, proactive, or productive. In the time some managers devote to worrying, a good leader would have things back on track and would have moved on to a new situation.

The farther you go down the leadership ladder in many organizations, the more people seem to worry. The men and women at the top don't have time for much worrying. If you're worrying a lot on the job about the job, what does this tell you?

Even if worrying could help prevent or handle setbacks, research says that most of us worry about the wrong things anyway. Here's the breakdown of what people (school administrators included) worry about:

Things that never happen	40%
Things beyond anyone's control	35%
Things that turn out better than expected	15%
Petty, useless things	8%
Legitimate concerns	2%

It seems that Richard Carlson's two rules of life are right after all:

1. Don't sweat the small stuff.

2. It's all small stuff.

Good leaders have known this all along. The odds are almost 50 to 1 against worries coming true, so effective leaders face their worries squarely, do something about them if they can, and refuse to worry about things that don't matter.

If you want to lose less and lead more, dump the worry habit. There are better ways to deal with setbacks.

WHAT IT TAKES TO BOUNCE BACK

Reversals and other unexpected glitches are the proving grounds for leadership. Nobody likes misfortune, but real leaders earn their stripes salvaging setbacks. The test and challenge of overcoming obstacles brings out the best in them.

Anyone can crumble when things go wrong. It takes some special skills and know-how, however, to bounce back. Today's winning principals and superintendents do it all the time. Nobody teaches a course in setback management, but ordinary mortals can learn how to do it just as well as most doctoral candidates.

Handling setbacks requires the ability to remain confident, maintain perspective, weigh options, make decisions, respond quickly, and pay attention to detail despite distraction. These are all learnable attributes.

If there ever is a time for leaders to mind their "Ps and Qs," it's during periods of setback. In these situations, "P" represents preparedness and "Q" stands for quickness. These are the watchwords for remedying reversals, minimizing any lasting negative effects, and restoring normalcy as soon as possible.

Broken bones often heal even stronger than before. The same thing can happen when things break down in a school or school system. If the leader deals successfully with problems or mistakes, the organization can grow from the experience and become even stronger, better, and more effective.

The time-honored strategies that work best for turning around bad situations and bouncing back after a setback are simply to accept, learn, and renew effort.

The best administrators accept setbacks as a normal part of doing business. They don't try to deny, rationalize, or cover up problems. They're not afraid to accept reality and responsibility, but they accept them with an attitude. It helps to be a little philosophical. Setbacks aren't just problems, they're also opportunities.

Once it's been acknowledged that something has gone wrong, the next step is to learn whatever lesson failure has to offer. Every setback has something to teach to all those involved.

Good leaders look for the lesson. They figure out what went wrong and why. What could have been done differently? Better? Sooner? They analyze cause and effect, ask the tough questions, and play out alternative scenarios. With experience, these become automatic responses.

Once the meaning of the setback has been mastered, it's time to let it go. As a leader, you can learn from every mistake, but you don't want to make it your entire curriculum.

After the facts have been accepted and the lessons learned, the next step is action. Renewed effort is always the best response to setbacks. Effective leaders redouble their efforts if necessary. They try harder. They find a way to make things right and to make things better. Keeping at it works every time.

These are the three measures that work best in settling setbacks. Of course, there are lots of other ways to react to reversals. Some help, and some don't. Most veteran administrators agree that the following behaviors top the list of additional things to do or avoid when events to wrong:

- "Fess up" if you did anything wrong. The sooner, the better.
- Remain calm. Control your emotions. Common sense is your best friend in times of trial.
- Be realistic about what you're facing. Determine how important the setback really is. Ask "Whose problem is it?" Adjust the level and intensity of your response to the degree of difficulty involved.
- Act like you're doing something to correct the situation (even if you're bluffing).
- Buy time to regain your composure. Take time out if you need it.
- Turn your attention (and others' attention) elsewhere until you figure out what to do. Give your subconscious mind time to work on the problem.
- Don't take setbacks personally. Just because bad things happen doesn't mean you are a bad leader or a bad person.
- Don't get stuck agonizing over what went wrong. A setback isn't a permanent retreat unless you stay there. The agony of defeat is real, but it shouldn't be forever. Get moving. Make something good happen to help everyone (including yourself) forget about the setback.
- Don't whine. Leadership isn't for crybabies. Pouting is for kids. Leaders are supposed to be adults. There are many worthwhile ways administrators can act when things go wrong. Being pathetic isn't one of them.
- Don't get mad, don't get even, just get back on track.
- Remember that response time is critical. Get active. Make things right as soon as possible. Plan a new course of action. Set new goals.

- Free others from guilt or blame.
- Don't make phony excuses. They're usually transparent. Besides, the school board and the public want action, not alibis.
- Don't apologize for trying something new even if it didn't work out. Pushing the envelope is part of every leader's job. The only people who never make mistakes are those who never do anything. Even that is a mistake.
- Keep things in perspective by remembering the good times in the bad times.
- Ask for help if you need it. Use your support network. That's what it's for.
- Don't give up on kids, on yourself, on the job, or on the future.
- Don't withdraw by just doing the minimum. This is the time to do more, not less.
- Retain your sense of humor. It's better to laugh at yourself than to cry over reversals.
- Keep your options open. Remember your "exit card." If the setback is bad enough, this may be the time to play it.

Leaders don't get to be leaders by handling smooth sailing. They get there by overcoming adversity. Setbacks are necessary rites of passage for leaders in all fields.

The best leaders also know that just making things right after a setback isn't enough. Attention also has to be paid to the leader's image; the organization's image; and the stakeholder's perception of what happened, how it was handled, and how things are now that it's over.

Damage control is an important part of dealing with setbacks. It never is right to lie about the situation, but it also never hurts to put the best possible face on the matter.

IS THERE A SPIN DOCTOR IN THE HOUSE?

Many administrators never even think about image issues during times of setback. They're just glad to live through the situation. By contrast, experienced leaders always think of attending to image. They understand that in times of stress and trial, perception isn't just as important as reality. It's more important.

We all know that professional politicians often hire image makers to put a positive spin on things when they get in trouble. Did you know, however, that really smart school leaders do much the same thing?

The difference is that schools don't have paid spin doctors (although the district communications coordinator or public relations specialist can help if you're lucky enough to have one). School officials have to do their own damage control.

Although certain politicians are willing to bend the truth and put a favorable spin on things for all the wrong reasons (e.g., to hide something, to hide behind, or to save their hides), school leaders tell the truth (they don't have to lie to find some good in a bad situation and put setbacks into perspective) and try to cast events in the best possible light for legitimate reasons, such as to

1. Ensure continued stakeholder confidence and support

2. Maintain momentum

3. Preserve credibility

4. Regenerate morale and enthusiasm

5. Keep as many doors open as possible for future advancement

When setbacks strike, the person in charge needs to be visible and set the pattern of response for others to follow. A leader's priorities when responding to setbacks or crises should always be to protect people, property, and image—in that order.

A leader's future success doesn't depend solely on the way he or she actually handles problems. It also hinges on how the leader communicates the problems and articulates how they were handled.

When leaders in any kind of organization communicate about problems or setbacks, it's usually not merely a random, unrehearsed act. Average administrators might speak off the cuff without considering trouble spots. Real leaders seldom do. They know that in order to put the best spin on a bad situation, the goals of all official communications regarding the problem should be to

- Provide reassurance ("Things are OK").
- Show genuine concern and evidence that the situation is being taken seriously.
- Accept responsibility (without necessarily admitting any real fault or guilt).
- Identify causes without engaging in shaming or blaming.
- Spell out the corrective measures that are under way.
- Underscore the lessons learned from the situation, the good that can come from it, and the measures being taken to prevent any reoccurrence.
- Praise the people who have handled the problem responsibly and professionally.
- Radiate and reestablish confidence ("We're on top of the situation now").
- Reaffirm the commitment to long-term goals.
- Give people something positive and exciting to look forward to.

Achieving these goals means that leaders have to get all of the facts quickly, commit to finding a solution, remain candid and positive, and focus on the future.

Information regarding any setback should be open and accessible. This requires establishing methods of communication with all affected parties and creating easy ways for people to get answers to all of their questions.

It shouldn't come as any surprise that damage control often begins and ends in the media. Setbacks in school plans or goof-ups by school administrators are news. The public will want answers, and the media will be trying to get them. Damage control frequently succeeds or fails in the headlines of the local newspaper or on the evening TV newscast.

If you want to succeed as a school leader and don't know anything about working with reporters, it's time you learned. There are good and bad ways of communicating with the media. What follows is a list of what a good leader should avoid in communicating with the media during a crisis.

The guidelines in the list below are used by professional spin doctors when dealing with the media, and they can work for you as well in times of setback.

To be proactive and get the jump on damage control, many mediawise administrators issue their own press releases. It's a mistake, however, to think that a press release will get you off the hook and protect you from answering reporters' questions. Sudden death is the only way to avoid facing interviews and responding to direct questioning.

How Self-Serving Politicians Try to Spin Setback Floss Into Survival Gold

- I don't know anything about it.
- It's not my fault.
- Someone else is to blame.
- It's not as bad as it looks.
- It's not what it appears to be.
- It's being taken care of.
- It's under investigation.
- I can't comment on it for reasons of privacy, confidentiality, or security.
- It's really a good thing.
- It's history.
- It never happened.
- It's a conspiracy.

How to Deal With the Media During
Setbacks, Crises, and Emergency Situations

- Be accessible.

- Never lie to media representatives.

- Don't bluff. If you don't know, admit it.

- Don't withhold information.

- Don't put off reporters. They have deadlines too.

- Keep promises to return calls to reporters.

- Tell bad news quickly. Get it over with.

- Don't hide behind "No comment."

- Limit comments to factual information. Avoid editorializing.

- Don't assume that anything is "off the record."

- Avoid using jargon. Plain talk works best.

- Give short, direct answers (the media thrive on sound bites).

- Be careful of making any libelous statements or violating confidentiality or privacy laws.

- Rehearse or role-play interviews in advance whenever possible.

- Hold a press conference if appropriate in order to get identical information to all news sources.

- Don't expect kid glove treatment. Some reporters are used to playing rough to get at the truth.

- If you're interviewed on TV, pay attention to dress, posture, and appearance. First impressions are the only impressions on a 60-second TV news report.

- Don't play favorites with reporters.

- Keep explanations simple. Complicated analyses get lost on the editing room floor.

- Don't be afraid to repeat the obvious. What's ordinary to you may be news to outsiders.

- Designate a single spokesperson to deal with all media.

To be effective, all press releases should be carefully written, tightly focused, and easy to read. The best press releases anticipate questions and cover all the bases. (Remember the goals for communicating during a setback.)

Press releases can be valuable tools for defusing setback situations, but media representatives don't always like them. Reporters don't want to feel used or manipulated. They want to get at the information they want, not just the information the organization wants to give them. Savvy leaders are prepared to provide both.

Image making and damage control are areas where many run-of-the-mill managers are no-shows. It never occurs to them to engage in these activities. Being a spin doctor isn't in the job description. Nevertheless, attending to image and putting the best face possible on a problem situation is a touch of class and finesse that separates genuine leaders from pretenders.

Sample News Release

NEWS RELEASE

For Immediate Release

Contact Person: _____

Phone No. _____

BOMB THREAT PANIC AVERTED

Thanks to quick action by school personnel, a bomb threat evacuation at _____High School was handled as a routine fire drill. Most students were unaware of anything out of the ordinary.

At 2 p.m. on Friday, the school office received an anonymous bomb threat. Following the school's predetermined emergency plan, students were quickly evacuated to a site a safe distance from the school while the police bomb squad searched the building and grounds for explosive devices. None were found.

Police officials credit the school's quick response time with avoiding any undue panic among students or staff members. This is the third bomb threat received by the school in the past 2 years. No actual bombs have been found to date, but each threat is taken seriously and handled according to district guidelines for emergency action.

"Most bomb threats are hoaxes, but they aren't a joke," explains Police Chief_____. "Anyone with information about this latest incident should contact city police immediately," the chief added.

Principal _____commented that today's unscheduled fire drill actually served as a wake-up call and a good introduction for next week's Fire Safety Program, which will involve all students in learning the latest fire prevention and emergency safety measures.

FEAR LESS, HOPE MORE

Setbacks can trigger fear, and fear is contagious. The worst possible result of any reversal is when it makes the leader afraid.

Fear is a major cause of leadership paralysis—the inability to make decisions and to take action. A fearful leader is no leader at all. Worse yet, fear is a thief of hope.

Hope is the greatest gift a leader can give any organization. Without hope for survival, hope for success, and hope for a better future, no organization can make it for long.

There is a reason why famed psychiatrist Karl Menninger called hope "the most powerful human emotion." Hope is a self-fulfilling prophecy and a force multiplier that can transform a school from mediocre to meteoric.

Good schools are rooted in a premise of hope. Without it, they are merely holding tanks for kids. And it should be no surprise that the one person who always has primary responsibility for keeping hope alive throughout any organization—especially a school—is the leader. ("A leader is a dealer in hope."—Napoleon Bonaparte).

Crepe hangers don't make good leaders. Realistic optimists do. The best leaders reject fear and embrace hope no matter what setbacks they encounter. They know the difference between caution and cowardice.

Good leaders believe that setbacks are only temporary. As the old saying goes, "This too shall pass." If you want to last as a leader, you can't allow reversals to make you afraid. When setbacks, emergencies, or crises occur, effective leaders fear less and hope more. If that's not a law, it should be!

BUILDING A REPUTATION AS A SURVIVOR

Surprisingly, surviving setbacks can even enhance your reputation as a leader. When you consistently overcome problems and disappointments, you build a reputation for strength. (No one remembers that it may have been you who screwed up in the first place.)

People rally around leaders who demonstrate that they can meet setbacks—even disasters—and still survive. Everyone loves the phoenix that rises from the ashes.

Every setback surmounted adds to the leader's image as a survivor. Over time, this reputation for surviving becomes an asset and an advantage in itself. The leader becomes more confident that setbacks can be overcome, and others gain faith that the leader is a survivor no matter what happens. This makes it easier to deal with subsequent reversals. In short, a leader's reputation for surviving past setbacks often becomes a tool for surviving future setbacks.

The 12 Worst Fears of Weak Leaders

1. Fear of failure

2. Fear of trying something new

3. Fear of trusting one's own judgment

4. Fear of ridicule

5. Fear of embarrassment

6. Fear of rejection

7. Fear of loss of respect

8. Fear of job loss

9. Fear of loss of power

10. Fear of loss of prestige

11. Fear of taking chances or risks

12. Fear of a tarnished image

Note: No priority order is implied.

Remember Tylenol after the infamous package-tampering incident? Or Bill (the "Comeback Kid") Clinton after the intern sex scandal? Or Nelson Mandela after years of imprisonment? Examples of individuals and organizations facing serious setbacks and coming out on top can be found around the world and across the street every day. It never happens by accident, however. It comes about as the result of an unflinching can-do attitude, an uncompromising willingness to learn from mistakes, and a doggedly persistent positive view of what's possible.

Knowing how to handle setbacks is a survival tool for today's administrators. Successful leaders have to bounce back from reversals great and small and still stay on course. Actually, they don't just bounce back, they come back stronger than ever. Resiliency isn't just an asset today. It's a necessity.

A setback is a bump in the road, not the end of the road, unless the leader stops there. Good leaders don't stop. The model leaders (principals and superintendents) you admire from the past are remembered for their hits (successes), not for their outs (setbacks). Leaders have more hits than other people because they have more at-bats. They keep coming back for more. It's called survival, and it's a way of life for successful leaders. It can become your way of living and working as well.

No one likes reversals, but good leaders make peace with them. There's a reason that many experts urge administrators, managers, and aspiring leaders in all fields to make friends with their problems: Without setbacks, there is no possibility for triumph.

8

Thinking Like a Leader

Everyone knows that leaders have to be doers. That's what they're hired for. If their efforts don't result in positive action, they aren't leading the organization anywhere. Nevertheless, leadership is still a thinking occupation, first and foremost.

The leader doesn't have to be the smartest person in the organization, but he or she has to be able to think clearly, recognize good thinking in others, access it when necessary, and use it effectively to reach personal and institutional goals.

Likewise, you don't have to be first in your class to become an effective principal or superintendent, but you do have to be able to think ahead and to think through problems. More importantly, you have to be willing to think. Many people—including some school administrators—have gotten out of the habit.

Fortunately, leaders don't all think alike. There is room for all types of thinkers at the top. Some leaders are concrete sequential thinkers. Others are radically random thinkers. Some stick to a linear process for problem solving. Others pursue a more circuitous, off-the-wall approach to finding solutions.

There's no one right way to think like a leader. Most thought processes, patterns, or habits can work as long as they are balanced by different ways of thinking on the part of other key people in the organization.

Even though they don't think identically, most effective leaders share the following common mental traits that set them apart from nonleaders.

- Leaders think more than most people do. They spend more time on and off the job thinking about possibilities, solutions, and future plans. A leader's life is a life of reflection. (If thinking could burn off calories, there would be very few overweight leaders.)
- Leaders plan to think. They value thinking, planning, and problem solving as legitimate and necessary leadership functions. They take time and make time for thinking without apology or embarrassment.
- Leaders think more about the needs of others (students, staff, parents, and community members) and of the organization as a whole than they do about themselves. They realize that their interests are best served by serving the interests of others.
- Leaders think more positively than many other people do. They see opportunities where others see only problems. They see new beginnings where others see dead ends. They look for possibilities, whereas others look for trouble.
- Leaders think more divergently than most others do. They think "out of the box" without any predetermined restraints limiting possible solutions. They look for new and different ways to do things.
- Leaders think ahead more than most people do. They live in the moment but constantly think ahead to tomorrow.

Many school administrators, stuck in a managerial mode, are as intelligent as any leader, but they don't think the same way. Most managers think about today and wonder what will happen tomorrow. Leaders think about what they want to happen tomorrow and then do what it takes today to bring it about. Successful leaders make it a habit to practice "anticipatory thinking" (which will be discussed shortly).

We all know quick-witted administrators in important leadership positions who think fast on their feet and respond quickly to circumstances. They may succeed for a while, but they seldom become great leaders. The great ones anticipate problems and make corrections in advance so that they don't have to resort to knee-jerk reactions under pressure. The better the leader, the fewer the surprises. Good leaders adopt a "preventive maintenance mentality." Anybody can do it, but most people just don't get around to it.

Leaders, in schools and elsewhere, don't necessarily think better or faster than anyone else. They are just more disciplined in focusing their thought processes. Mental discipline, like physical discipline, is a learned behavior. No one is born with it.

We now know that all kids can benefit from being taught higher-level thinking skills. These skills are not just for gifted kids anymore. All students can learn to incorporate analysis, synthesis, and evaluation to some degree into their everyday thinking. If kids can learn these thinking skills, surely you can learn to think like a leader. It starts by forcing yourself to consistently think beyond the present.

ANTICIPATORY THINKING: GETTING THE JUMP ON PROBLEMS

The best leaders in all fields are proactive, not merely reactive. This applies to thinking as well as to action. Good leaders routinely think ahead; plan in advance; try to forecast developments; play out possible, probable, and preferable scenarios in their minds; figure out where current conditions are leading; and anticipate how people may react to alternative courses of action. It's called anticipatory thinking.

The advantage is that it allows leaders to solve problems ahead of time and to act before they are forced to or told to. It's not magic, and it's not science, but it is an effective way to get the jump on trouble before it happens.

The following three easy examples illustrate the edge that this kind of thinking can provide:

1. If help is going to be needed, the leader can begin to line it up well in advance.

2. If a project is going to be a "hard sell," the leader can initiate a marketing plan early.

3. If an approach is going to take too much time, the leader can switch to a different plan before it's too late.

Anticipatory thinking is a mental habit, just as dwelling in the past or thinking only in the moment is a habit. Fortunately, habits can be formed, broken, and reformed. That's what growth is all about.

Adopting the habit of anticipatory thinking is one of the first steps in moving away from simply plugging along as a make-do manager to becoming a full-fledged, can-do leader.

The way to start shifting into an anticipatory thinking mode is to do what the futurists do. Read lots of newspapers and professional journals, stay in touch with the latest research, pay attention to what's happening in other schools, and keep your antenna tuned to new ideas and promising practices. Spot trends in the making, and try to extrapolate possible future developments and directions.

With a little effort and practice, most administrators find that it's just as easy to get into the habit of thinking ahead as it is to habitually concentrate on the past or present.

Another way to start acquiring the anticipatory thinking habit is to make tough self-questioning part of your regular thought process. Make playing 20 questions (or more) the way you do business in your head. Ask yourself enough of the right questions and you'll routinely come up with the right answers before other people do. That's anticipatory thinking. It's also leadership at its best.

Anticipatory Thinking Questions

Asking yourself these kinds of questions can help you shift into a forward-thinking mind-set.

What's going to happen?

What if . . . ?

What is needed? Why?

What would it take to . . . ?

What will work?

What else will work?

What will work best?

What will make it work?

What are the steps involved?

How do we start?

When do we start?

What do we have to do now?

What do I need to prepare for?

How will people react?

Who can help? Who will help?

Who will resist? How?

What can go wrong?

What will keep things from going wrong?

What don't we know that we need to know? Who will benefit most? Least? How?

What are the possible surprises?

What's likely to change? How soon? How much?

What if we do nothing?

What is the worst-case scenario?

Should something else take precedence?

What do we do if the worst-case scenario really happens?

Is it possible? What are the odds?

Is it practical?

Is the timing right?

Is it ethical?

Is it worth it?

Does it feel right?

How can we make it more fun?

What if we fail?

What's Plan B?

Someone has to do advanced thinking for every organization. If not the leader, who else? Anticipatory thinking is just another tool that effective leaders use to discern where they want the organization to go and why. It also helps them maintain perspective and stay mentally focused on the big picture.

WHAT TO DO WHEN THE BIG PICTURE IS A KALEIDOSCOPE

Administrators who are content to perform routine housekeeping functions can afford to think only about their daily tasks and their specific area of responsibility. Real leaders cannot.

Leaders are expected to keep the big picture in mind. They have to think beyond the immediate and consider the organization as a whole, how it fits into the greater world, and how its various pieces (e.g., curriculum, instruction, staff development, budgeting, communications, etc.) interact and mesh with each other.

People are supposed to see more and better from the top. The view is better from up there. Street-smart leaders know that if they don't see farther than most, they won't stay at the top very long.

The problem today is that there is no clear-cut, consistent big picture anymore. Expectations, demands, requirements, values, priorities, circumstances, and possibilities are constantly changing. Lines have been blurred. Pigeonholes have disappeared. Very little remains distinct or definite anymore. Nothing stands still. Reality can be turned upside down almost overnight. Glance away for a moment, and the whole world may be reconfigured. Change is not only inevitable. It is incessant.

No longer can a leader get a firm grasp of the big picture. There isn't any. Today, the big picture has become a kaleidoscope of rapidly changing snapshots.

What, then, are leaders supposed to do in a kaleidoscopic world? How are they supposed to think and act? The alternatives are clear:

1. Continue to do what leaders have always done best.

2. Give up.

3. Go crazy.

The best choice is obvious. Even with a continuously shifting big picture, effective school leaders have to continue to plan, try, test, adjust, and plan again as they always have. Only now, they need to build in more flexibility, contingencies, back-up plans, and fallback positions. Modern leaders have to think more about adaptability than their predecessors did.

An adaptive school culture is not only best suited for today's uncertain times, it is the only kind of organization that will survive. Adaptability isn't a natural state. It is the result of old-fashioned divergent thinking and careful planning.

Despite tumultuous paradigm shifts and a mind-boggling information explosion, good leaders still need to think and act like leaders. Sound thinking, logic, and common sense never go out of style.

It's better to approach chaos with a plan (better yet, with several plans) than to face it unprepared. With a well-thought-out plan passionately pursued, even chaos can be controlled—or at least managed.

Visioning, goal setting, and strategic planning still work. They just need a few modern twists. Besides using anticipatory thinking more than in the past, successful leaders in today's schools and businesses have to apply more multiscenario thinking and work harder to stay focused in the face of distractions.

MULTISCENARIO THINKING

Television manufacturers knew what they were doing when they invented the picture-in-a-picture set allowing viewers to see more than one program at once. There's too much going on for busy viewers to watch only one channel at a time.

Effective leaders have to think much the same way today. (The mind can work like a split-screen TV set if we tell it to.) They have to consider several options and possibilities at the same time. Some educators call it "multiscenario thinking." If you can hold more than one picture in your mind at a time, you can do it too.

Because things are in a constant state of flux and conditions refuse to remain stable, no leader can rely on a single blueprint for the future anymore. Principals and superintendents now have to visualize and weigh several possibilities simultaneously. Today's leaders have to think about what might work, what they hope will work, what they think will work, and what to do if none of it works—all at the same time. If you can do that, you're thinking like a leader.

Considering a variety of approaches together gives a leader multiple tools and multiple choices. It provides the person in charge with more flexibility and promotes eclectic leadership (adapting and applying whatever works best in each given situation).

Multiscenario thinking is the best bet for dealing with today's fragmented and frenetic world. That's why genuine leaders like to tackle problems in more than one way, whereas managers stick to tried-and-true approaches no matter what.

If you want to sharpen your multiscenario thinking skills, the following tips and exercises can help:

- Visualize several ways to reach a goal before committing to any one approach.
- Draw up a mental list of possibilities, and hold an internal debate on the pros and cons of each.
- Don't settle for the first idea that comes along. Keep digging. Keep probing.
- Make it your own personal rule to consider at least three ways to do a task.
- Be open-minded enough to absorb many points of view—including those of competitors or antagonists.

Anything that broadens your horizons, introduces new ways of doing or thinking about things, or creates fresh alternatives can help make you a better multiscenario thinker. The trick, then, is to stay focused on desired goals while playing out numerous competing options and fending off distractions from all directions.

HOW TO STAY FOCUSED

If there is one distinguishing feature that separates winning leaders from losers and also-rans, it must be the capacity to stay focused. Leaders know how to keep their eye on the ball. They refuse to forget why they became educators.

Focus is particularly crucial during kaleidoscopic times of chronic change and perpetual distraction. If the leader loses sight of the destination, the whole organization can get lost.

Everyone in the organization has a job. The leader's is to keep reminding everyone of their purpose (mission, vision, goals) and, somehow, to keep things generally moving in the right direction. Anyone else can wander off course and the rest of the organization won't follow, but when the leader is lost, all is lost—at least for a while.

Most leaders in all fields think differently from other people primarily because they are more focused than others. The critical reason for remaining focused no matter what is to ensure that energy is invested in things that really matter and to avoid wasting resources on marginal or tangential efforts that don't make a difference in the long run. Leaders focus their thinking on results, not just on activity.

For educators, this simply means that effective school leaders consistently focus organizational energy and attention on improving the basic conditions of learning, which J. Villars and other researchers refer to as "PSSSSST," an acronym for Purpose, Students, Strategies, Stuff (materials), Staff, Space, and Time.

Some schools build a dynasty of athletic championships and think they're doing a good job. Others build a dynasty of academic champions and know they're doing a good job. Guess which ones have principals and other leaders who are truly focused on the mission of the school?

The old adage that "managers concentrate on doing things right, whereas leaders focus on doing the right thing" isn't just a clever play on words. It's a one-sentence sermon on what focused leadership is all about.

In a world where change is measured in nanoseconds, it's not easy to stay focused on anything. There are too many distractions, too many forces competing for attention, and too many attractive nuisances along the way. It's no wonder that some schools end up drifting or lost.

That's why many leaders are willing to do almost anything, including using quirky reminders (like PSSSSST), to keep the organization focused on the real reason for being in business. Good leaders are never too proud to use gimmicks to keep their focus intact, and you won't be either if you want to think like a leader. Here's what some successful principals and superintendents have tried with good results:

• Memorize the mission statement. Make it your mantra. Recite it. Repeat it often. Invoke it whenever the big picture gets more fuzzy or confused than usual.

• Use sticky notes to saturate your personal spaces (i.e., your home, office, and car) with reminders of long- and short-term goals and priorities. (Don't forget to use refrigerator magnets and bathroom mirror memos to remind yourself.)

• Place banners and posters containing the mission statement and key results in strategic locations throughout the school or district.

• Print up billfold-size cards with the school's belief statements and distribute them to all personnel.

• Train staff members to help each other stay focused by constantly asking one another, "Is it good for kids?"

• Take a tip from syndicated columnist Mark Stevens and create a personal organizer designed to help keep you focused on key tasks by (a) listing what you want to achieve in the next week, (b) prioritizing the list, (c) creating a headline for the list that defines your most important objective, (d) reviewing the list at the end of each day to see what's been accomplished, and (e) revising the list for the next day.

You can never become an effective school leader until you learn to stay focused when most others around you are rattled, confused, or lost. ("Keep your head while others around you are losing theirs.") There are no distractible leaders. It's a contradiction in terms. Focus is just one of several mental habits that separate real leaders from imitations.

THE 7 HABITS OF HIGHLY EFFECTIVE SCHOOL LEADERS, WITH APOLOGIES TO STEPHEN COVEY

School administrators should borrow a page from their counterparts in business by reading more of the growing body of professional literature on the subject of leadership. By now, most self-respecting business executives have read Stephen Covey's groundbreaking work *The 7 Habits of Highly Effective People* at least once. Some school officials haven't even heard of it, let alone read it.

Covey is recognized as a pioneer in the business community for spelling out the critical thinking and behavioral habits that set apart the most effective leaders in all fields. His work has become a must-read classic for serious leaders in all areas of business. If you're not familiar with it, you're missing an opportunity to gain some powerful insight into what makes leaders tick.

What Covey says about business applies equally to school systems. It should be no surprise that the habits of highly effective people in business that Covey wrote about turn out to be the habits of highly effective school leaders as well.

With apologies for some serious oversimplification, the leadership habits identified by Covey as they apply to school administration are listed below. If you want to think like a leader, these make a good place to start:

1. *Be proactive.* According to Covey, effective people recognize the need to change from the inside out and constantly strive to create their own destiny. Doesn't this sound a lot like creating a vision for the school and working to attain it? The best principals and superintendents you know have always thought proactively.

2. *Begin with the end in mind.* Effective people forgo quick fixes and evaluate the significance of their actions in relation to how much they move the organization toward its vision. That's why successful school leaders don't buy into every new fad that comes along. Real leaders aren't trendy. They're more interested in timeless goals and lasting results.

3. *Put first things first.* Effective people manage their time so that they can put important things first and say no to other things. They make a habit of thinking about values first. Good school leaders are no different. They "walk their talk." They incorporate belief statements into the school's long-range plan. Effective school leadership has always been value based and principle centered (see Chapter 12 in this book).

4. *Think win/win.* Effective people seek mutually beneficial solutions. Good school leaders do the same thing, whether it's making curriculum

decisions, resolving discipline problems, or negotiating a master contract. In good schools, there are no winners or losers. It's the leader's job to see that it works out that way.

5. *Seek first to understand and then to be understood.* Covey says that effective business leaders diagnose before they prescribe. It works the same way in schools. The most successful and admired school leaders think first about what the other person has to say and then about what they want to say. They listen more and talk less than many other people. Have you ever known a great principal or superintendent who wasn't a good listener?

6. *Synergize.* Effective people habitually think about making new connections and combinations and creating new alternatives so that the whole can function as more than the sum of its parts. Today's school leaders have to think this way. Piecemeal thinking yields only partial answers. That's why departmental organizations are being replaced by interdisciplinary teams in many schools.

7. *Sharpen the saw.* Effective people make it a habit to think about and care for themselves first in order to make all the other habits possible. They invest in renewing themselves physically, mentally, professionally, and spiritually. They watch TV less and exercise, read, write, meditate, and perform community service more than most people. Outstanding school executives have done this all along. If this doesn't sound like your principal or superintendent, it should. Workaholics don't make the best school leaders. Well-rounded, healthy individuals do.

Covey is right. Leaders with these habits are more effective than leaders without them. If you haven't developed these habits already, they make a wonderful list of self-improvement goals to work on. It's pretty hard to possess these traits and not be an effective school leader.

MORE AIDS TO CLEAR THINKING

Besides working on Covey's seven habits, there are lots of other ways to develop the clear thinking skills necessary to be a successful leader in today's schools. Here are some of the best techniques for becoming a better thinker (and a better leader at the same time):

- Screen information, but don't wait until you have all possible data before making a decision. That will never happen. Strike a balance between too much and too little information.
- Remember that clear thinking is decisive thinking. It moves toward action. Thinking is a step, not the whole process. Leaders have to be doers too.
- Use higher-level thinking skills as much as possible.

Bloom's Taxonomy of Higher-Level Thinking Skills

1. Knowledge level

2. Comprehension level

3. Application level

4. Analysis level

5. Synthesis level

6. Evaluation level

- Look for similarities of current problems to past problems, and remember previous solutions. There's no law against repeating success.
- Always watch out for new connections, opportunities, and possibilities.
- Apply holistic thinking. Try to think with both sides of your brain. Neither has a monopoly on truth or wisdom.
- Be suspicious of easy answers to difficult questions.
- If you're stuck for an answer, reframe the question.

Holistic Thinking

Left-Brain Functions	Right-Brain Functions
Rational cognition	Intuition
Logic	Fantasy
Analysis	Imagination
Objectivity	Subjectivity
Linear thinking	Creative thinking

- Use feedback to provoke deeper thought. Try out ideas on others. Think out loud. Evaluate reactions.
- Seek out best practices and make them your own.
- Remember that not all intelligence is measured by an IQ score. Apply different kinds of intelligence to solve different kinds of problems.
- Avoid "ideacide" (killing off other people's good ideas). Reward good thinking wherever you find it.
- Build reality checks into your thinking.
- Listen to what opponents have to say. Think about their ideas. It pays to weigh competing views.
- Don't forget to ask "So what?" and "Who cares?"

Alternative Intelligences (A Partial List)

Linguistic intelligence

Mathematical intelligence

Visual, puzzle-solving intelligence

Kinesthetic intelligence

Emotional intelligence

Social intelligence

Common sense intelligence

- When everything else is equal, always pick the least complicated solutions.
- Let your subconscious do part of the thinking for you.
- Look for ways to solve two problems with one solution.
- Try to think unfettered. What seems like a crazy idea at first may prove to be a good solution in the long run.
- Remember that how you think about your job shapes how you think on the job. Managers see their job as cut and dried. Good leaders view their job as a creative one.

You can learn to think like a leader if you want to. It's mostly a matter of practice and will. Leadership requires disciplined thinking, not genius. It also helps to know that you don't have to do it all by yourself.

The biggest mistake many would-be leaders make is to think that they have to do all the thinking for the organization. They don't. If you really want to think like the most effective school leaders, you'll think of ways to let those better and smarter than you do your thinking for you.

9

Looking and Acting Like an Effective School Leader

Image isn't everything, but sometimes it's all people have to go on. It's tempting to say that appearances don't count or aren't important, but successful leaders know better. If you look and act like a leader, it's a lot easier to be perceived as a leader, to be accepted as a leader, and, in fact, to actually be a leader. (When you look the part, you're more likely to get the part.)

It's true that what's inside a leader (e.g., brains, heart, guts, backbone, and soul) is more important than what's on the outside. Nevertheless, it doesn't make any difference if no one ever gets close enough to find out what's inside because a negative image gets in the way.

All retailers appreciate the importance of packaging. Even the best product may not survive if it isn't appropriately packaged so that potential buyers recognize it, remember it, and are willing to give it a chance. This same principle applies to becoming or surviving as a school leader.

Your image isn't something mysterious or ethereal. It's simply how you package yourself. It may spell the difference between getting the chance to lead and getting left out.

You might argue that reacting to people based on outward appearances isn't fair, and you probably would win the argument but still lose out as a leader. Reality isn't known for fairness. The best leaders don't argue about having to pay attention to packaging: they just do it.

WALK LIKE A DUCK

There used to be an old saying in vaudeville that "If it looks like a duck, walks like a duck, and quacks like a duck, it is a duck." This is the way many people think about their leaders. What you wear, how you look, and how you act is often more important than what you know.

Some administrators think it's phony to worry about polishing up their image. Savvy leaders understand that it's just part of the deal.

The more closely you resemble people's perception of a leader, the more likely they are to let you be a leader, take you seriously as a leader, respect you as a leader, and believe you to be a leader (and the more likely you are to believe it yourself as well).

How you come across is important. Fortunately, image is one thing you can do something about. So what are you waiting for?

IMAGE CONTROL

Most people (including many would-be school leaders) plan everything in their lives except their image. Sometimes, that can be a career-altering mistake. Image makes a difference. If you change your image, you can change your life forever. Don't let anyone tell you differently.

The good news is that only you can control your image. You can dress and behave like a slob if you want to. Likewise, looking and acting like a leader is a choice. You are your own image maker. If the impression you make on others isn't what you want it to be, you can reinvent your image at any time. It's not as hard as many people think, and it can be a lot of fun.

How you present yourself can change your behavior and that of those around you. If you change the way you see yourself, you'll change the way you act. If you change the way others see you, you will change the way they treat you and react to you as well.

Teachers have always known that the better students dress, the better they behave. Teachers themselves changed their image when they went from wearing dresses or suits and ties to more casual, informal wear. They gained comfort but sacrificed some respect and professional mystique. Parents, students, and the general public treat teachers differently now.

The old slogan "dress for success" still rings true. If you dress a little better (more appropriately), you'll look better, feel better, and usually perform better. It's possible to dress up your attitude and your act in the same way with the same results.

Your image is simply the sum total of how people see you and how you come across to them. It's like an instant reputation that you didn't have to earn. Nationally recognized personal development consultant Susan Morem has made it even clearer by identifying the five key components that make up a person's public image:

1. Impression

2. Movement

3. Attitude

4. Grooming

5. Etiquette

If you want to look and act more like an effective school leader, these are the areas on which you should work.

Obviously, there is no single image that is mandatory for all leaders, but there are some parameters worth noting and respecting.

People will be accepted and respected as leaders more quickly and easily if the way they dress, behave, and present themselves falls within the norms of the culture of the organization they are trying to lead. (What works for the leader of a biker gang won't work for a school principal or superintendent.) If you want to be readily perceived as a leader, your appearance and demeanor should fit in.

You don't have to lose your individuality or become a carbon copy of everyone else to be perceived as a leader, but you do need to be credible and believable. The goal is to make a favorable impression that sets you apart as a leader and makes it easy and comfortable for others to see you in a leadership role.

Some people think that image making is about spending a lot of money on clothes, accessories, and a makeover. They're missing the point. A positive, professional image is the result of good taste and good sense, not huge expenditures.

It doesn't cost much just to avoid an outdated look or to wear clean clothes that fit. Likewise, good grooming and good posture are free. So are civility, politeness, and poise. Learning how to look and act like a leader is a low-cost investment that can yield a big payoff.

The best ways to develop a leadership image are to notice how other leaders in your field look, act, and present themselves and to get advice and feedback from knowledgeable people you trust and respect. Don't be afraid to role-play or hold a dress rehearsal before going public with a new image.

Just paying attention is all you really have to do to find out how to look and act like a leader. It doesn't take X-ray vision to see what works and what doesn't.

THERE'S NO ONE RIGHT WAY TO ACT—BUT THERE ARE LOTS OF WRONG WAYS

Most business and professional leaders practice moderation in appearance and behavior. If anything, they err on the conservative side.

Of course, there are always exceptions. We can all point to a few leaders who break all the rules and still come out on top. There are successful leaders who sport weird hairdos, boast tattoos, wear rings in strange places, or flaunt outrageous costumes. Such leaders succeed in spite of their image, not because of it. Their persona makes it harder, rather than easier, for others to trust and treat them as leaders. If you want to be pragmatic and increase the odds of becoming a believable school leader, dare to look and act the part. It's not worth it to waste your nonconformity on trifles.

There's a lot more to maintaining a professional image than wearing a "power suit." Many looks, mannerisms, and behaviors immediately project an impression of authority and confidence. Other ways of dressing and acting do just the opposite (e.g., slouching and shuffling don't come across as images of leadership capability).

Successfully presenting yourself as a leader depends as much on what you don't do as on what you do. You don't have to be a charm school graduate to come across as a leader, but you should at least be smart enough to avoid the common image busters below. Most people decide rather quickly that they're not dealing with an authentic leader when they see the person

- Showing off or bragging too much
- Monopolizing the conversation
- Being rude or crude
- Demanding to be the center of attention
- Exhibiting bigotry
- Bossing people around (Have you noticed lately that the best leaders get their own coffee?)
- Being confrontational, combative, or argumentative
- Drinking too much
- Overdoing makeup or gaudy jewelry and accessories
- Gossiping or feeding the rumor mill
- Making fun of others
- Expecting to be waited on
- Not listening
- Trying to be cute or flippant at other people's expense
- Making sexist remarks
- Ignoring personal hygiene
- Acting like he or she doesn't care
- Being angry and out of control
- Flirting with someone else's spouse or companion
- Being too busy for people who aren't "important"
- Showing disrespect for local culture, customs, and values

Those who merely want to get along as administrators may not have to worry so much about all of these niceties of behavior, but anyone who wants to emerge as a make-a-difference leader can't ignore them. One of the surest signs of leadership potential is a willingness to prepare adequately. This includes demonstrating self-discipline or doing whatever else it takes to develop an acceptable public image.

Avoiding inappropriate behaviors such as those outlined above may seem complicated and difficult. It really isn't. There are just two basic, commonsense rules: Boorish behavior is never "in," and outrageous or outlandish appearance and behavior are always "out." Projecting a positive, professional image just means being on your best behavior—looking and acting your best. (Would any real leader ever do less?)

Although making a favorable impression isn't as difficult as many think, there are obviously lots of ways to screw up your image. That's another reason for enlisting friends, colleagues, or mentors to give you honest feedback on how you're doing and then really listening to what such sympathetic critics have to say. No one has to put together their well-rounded professional image all by themselves.

MAINTAINING A PROFESSIONAL EDGE

If there is one word that describes the kind of image an effective leader wants to project, it's "professional." Coming across as a professional means radiating an aura of confidence and an air of competence. It's an attitude.

Principals and superintendents who appear professional have an edge over other administrators because their appearance and behavior are disciplined and carefully controlled. Professionals are perceived as can-do people who are always on top of the situation. They keep their attitudes, emotions, and actions in check. (For example, professionals manage their anger because they know that when they become angry, someone else is in control of the situation.)

The common dictionary definition of a *professional* is a "qualified, skilled practitioner or expert with considerable training and specialized study." If your goal is to become an effective school leader, this is the image you want to project.

Part of any professional image is mannerly conduct. If you want to be perceived as a credible and acceptable leader, it pays to dust off some of the etiquette and social skills your mother tried to teach you years ago.

MANNERS STILL MATTER

In today's kaleidoscopic world where rudeness has become commonplace, civility is making a comeback. There are growing signs that etiquette is returning to fashion among leaders in both the public and private sectors. More and more leaders are rediscovering that good manners are an important component of effective leadership.

Profile of a Professional

- Knowledgeable
- Organized
- Attentive
- Rational
- Thoughtful
- Self-assured
- Enthusiastic
- Focused
- Sense of humor
- Goal oriented
- Comfortable with self and others
- Takes others' problems seriously

- Active listener (all consummate professionals are good listeners)
- Enjoys problem solving and decision making
- Objective
- Responsible
- Responsive
- Tactful
- Courteous
- Optimistic
- Concerned
- Motivated
- Respectful
- Service oriented

Even many business schools across the country are now including a short course in manners as part of the required training for leaders-in-the-making. In some organizations, etiquette manuals are now joining texts on leadership theory as suggested reading for ambitious managers. Politeness has regained legitimacy as a leadership tool. If you're smart, you'll make it part of your professional image.

Like professionalism, etiquette is a mind-set (an attitude). People like to work with leaders who show respect and treat others with civility. Manners still matter.

If you're a principal or superintendent who still thinks manners are beneath you, you need to think again. The whole purpose of etiquette and well-mannered behavior is to help people feel more comfortable and confident because they understand the rules of acceptable behavior and know how to act and react in sensitive public situations.

Comfortable people perform better, and it is easier to do business with them. That's why social skills are becoming increasingly important for leaders in all fields. A little earthiness is still OK, but no one wants a slob or a boor for a leader. If you're going to get ahead as a school leader today, you're going to have to master a modicum of etiquette.

Surprisingly, good manners aren't for the faint of heart. It takes a certain amount of courage and discipline to break bad habits, control inappropriate responses, and hold your tongue in tense situations. With a little training, practice, and effort, however, anyone can learn how.

Etiquette isn't as silly, phony, or stuffy as some principals and superintendents assume it is. It can equip leaders with essential social competencies so that they can relax and make others relax, gain acceptance and respect, perform at their peak, and get the job done.

Good manners are mostly a matter of showing respect and applying good judgment. It bears repeating that moderation is usually the key to socially acceptable behavior and to making a favorable impression.

You don't have to know everything about etiquette to be perceived and treated as an effective leader, but you should know how to stick to certain time-honored standards. Most experts agree that the following examples represent the kinds of social behaviors needed by all leaders:

- Remember that posture is important. Stand straight. Sit straight. Slumping isn't a leadership position.
- Dress for the season (e.g., don't wear white shoes in winter unless you want your feet to blend in with the snow).
- Be prepared to converse about diverse topics—not just schools, kids, and sports.
- Pass food to the left.
- Pace your eating. Meals and races are separate events. There are no trophies for finishing first at a business luncheon or banquet.
- Save intimate questions for only very close friends.
- Remember what a handkerchief and tissue are for.
- Stay away from discussing sensitive subjects with people you don't know.
- Don't interrupt other people.
- Leave your chewing gum at home.
- Remember that eating with others is supposed to be sociable, not noisy (slurping and belching don't constitute acceptable dinner table conversation).
- Don't put your briefcase on someone else's table or desk.
- Avoid whispering or telling insider jokes that make others feel left out.
- Rise when someone new joins your party.
- Resist patronizing others.
- Remember that "please" and "thank you" are always in style—even for leaders.
- Don't correct other people's bad manners in public.

Your manners are like your wardrobe. They don't have to be perfect, but they need to be good enough to allow you to be accepted in every public situation without looking foolish, being uncomfortable, giving the impression that you don't belong, or jeopardizing your image as a leader. Good manners don't guarantee success, but bad manners are a sure-fire way to make a bad impression. Fortunately, it's never too late to learn proper etiquette. Why not start now?

Good manners are just one of the many little things that make up the way you come across to others. To look and act like a leader, you have to be willing to manage lots of details.

PAYING ATTENTION TO THE LITTLE THINGS THAT MARK A LEADER

When it comes to image building, the devil is in the detail. It's easy to do lots of big things right and still have a few minor glitches or flaws wreck the entire impression you're trying to create. For example, you might wear a perfectly tailored new suit, and all some people would notice are your dirty fingernails; or you might give a brilliant speech only to find out that all some people heard were a few innocent mispronunciations or grammatical errors. Details count.

In developing your image as a leader, you never have it right until you have it *all* right. Image is mostly minutiae compounded daily. Good leaders are known for their thoroughness and attention to details in their personal affairs. This applies to their public persona and demeanor as well.

Some administrators are totally oblivious to the little things that detract from a favorable image, and yet they wonder why they never get the respect and support they need to become the leader they wish they were. It's hardly worth explaining to them. Awareness is a test of leadership. These administrators fail before they start.

It might help if all prospective or aspiring leaders were required to memorize this old saying of Benjamin Franklin's:

For want of a nail, the shoe was lost.

For want of a shoe, the horse was lost.

For want of a horse, the rider was lost.

For want of a rider, the battle was lost.

For want of a battle, the war was lost.

Little things can make a big difference. If you want to come across as a leader, be a stickler for detail. Pay attention to the whole package. You don't want to lose points over inconsequential matters.

Following are 20 of the most common "little things" that set leaders apart and frequently make or break a favorable impression.

1. *Smile.* A great smile is the best introduction. That's why sourpusses seldom make good first impressions (or good leaders, for that matter). There's a reason that political leaders smile a lot. It works.

Smiling gets people on your side. It's contagious. Start an epidemic. You will always make a favorable impression, and you will be more readily perceived as leadership material at the same time.

Remember that the most beautiful smile is a genuine smile. Use yours often.

2. *Shoes.* Their shoes are the last thing some leaders think about, but they are the first thing many people look at. Scruffy shoes are always bad news for your image as a leader. It doesn't take much time, money, or effort to keep your shoes shined. Put your best foot forward and bolster your image by taking good care of your footwear.

3. *Stance.* People expect their leaders to stand erect. Don't disappoint them. Stooping, sprawling, and slouching aren't leadership postures. Stand straight and tall no matter how short you are. It's another way to look like a leader.

4. *Handshake.* Your handshake is literally the first impression you make on people. Make it a good one. Do you know any respected school leaders who have either a limp-wristed or a bone-crushing handshake? Think about it. A firm handshake sends a message of authority, confidence, and strength. Get a grip on leadership by developing a leader's handshake.

5. *Voice.* It's not enough just to look and act like a leader. Part of a winning image is sounding like one as well. A shrill or whiny voice doesn't help. Talking too fast also leaves listeners behind. Listen to yourself. Pay attention to the tone of your voice and your rate of speech. You can control how others hear you. Don't talk yourself out of being perceived as a leader.

6. *Bad breath.* Nothing blows a favorable impression faster than halitosis. There's no excuse for it. Breath mints and sprays are inexpensive. Don't leave home without them.

7. *Eye contact.* In our culture, direct eye contact signals respect, interest in the other person, and a lack of intimidation. Conversely, looking down or away or averting eye contact is taken as a sign of weakness, timidity, or lack of self-confidence. That's why effective leaders, like entertainers, use lots of eye contact. If making eye contact doesn't feel natural or comfortable, practice will help. Leaders connect with people, reach out to them, and touch them in many ways. Sometimes, they use their hands. Sometimes, they use only their eyes.

8. *Small talk.* Leaders shouldn't talk all the time, but they do need to be able to converse with people at all levels on multiple topics. Being able to carry on small talk is a skill worth cultivating. Identifying safe topics to talk about and rehearsing a little in advance make it a lot easier. If you can speak with ease and put others at ease, you've gone a long way toward building a solid image as a leader.

9. *Gestures.* Used properly, gestures enhance communication. This is why effective public speakers often practice in front of a mirror. Similarly, all leaders need to be aware of the impact of their gestures. Tiny gestures indicate hesitancy and tentativeness. On the other hand, a wild flailing of the arms only scares people off. The old rule of moderation applies.

10. *Body language.* Sometimes, body language speaks louder than words. Most people don't think about it, but tuned-in leaders are aware that the messages they send with their bodies are an important part of their image.

You don't have to be a linguist to read body language. Everyone knows the code (e.g., crossed arms indicate defensiveness, protectiveness, withdrawal, and/or a closed attitude, whereas leaning forward suggests interest, attentiveness, and concern. If you want to make a favorable impression, choose your body language as carefully as you choose your words.

11. *Grammar.* Using correct grammar is a sign of at least modest intelligence and a reasonable amount of education. Would anyone want less in a leader? Especially in a school principal or superintendent?

Like it or not, your grammar is part of your image. You don't need to know all of the rules to speak like a leader, but you do need an ear for what sounds right. If grammar is an area of weakness, it's worth going back to school. A good English or speech teacher can help.

For starters, any leader who wants to be taken seriously should learn that "uh" is not an acceptable part of speech used to punctuate every pause, and that "you know" is not a necessary ending for every sentence.

12. *Voice mail and e-mail etiquette.* Modern technology has added a new dimension to image making. Now, you not only make an impression on people in person but on the computer screen and on the telephone answering machine as well. Voice mail and e-mail aren't toys, but tools. They can be used to help people perceive you as a leader (or to reinforce the impression that you are not one). Like any tools, voice mail and e-mail can be overused, underused, misused, or abused. It happens in almost every workplace (including schools) every day, and managers and administrators are often the worst offenders. What's needed is some commonsense etiquette for using these tools like a leader.

The best leaders in businesses and in schools today follow the same rules of courtesy and consideration (etiquette) in using voice mail and e-mail as in all other dealings with people. Common sense and good manners work just as well when recorded as in person.

13. *Punctuality.* Not all leaders are habitually on time, but most of the really good ones are. Punctuality is a sign of respect. Making people wait makes them feel used. That's not a good impression for a leader to make.

14. *Seating arrangements.* There's no sitting down on the job when it comes to image making. Even when seated, a leader is on view. Where you sit and how you sit leaves an impression just as does everything else you do in public.

If you want to be thought of as a leader, do not sit in the back of the room. Sit where you will be noticed. Sit erect. Posture isn't just important when you're standing. Women wearing skirts always need to be conscious of modesty—particularly when sitting on a stage. Just sitting is easy. Sitting so you look like a leader takes a little extra time and thought. That's what leaders do—take the time to do the little things right.

15. *Names.* The single most important thing you can do to make a favorable impression and win the hearts of present subordinates and future followers is to remember their names. People's names are important to them. If you don't remember their names, they feel that you don't think they are important. The reason so many of us forget names isn't because of poor memory. It's laziness. People who are good at remembering names aren't smarter than others, they just work harder at it. The secret is to make name recall a priority. A few tricks can help, too: listen, really pay attention, repeat, make associations, and reuse the name as soon and as often as you can. Most administrators are lousy with names. The few great ones, however, do well at it. You will, too, if you want to pass ordinary and reach for remarkable.

16. *Smoking.* Using cigarettes—or even smokeless tobacco—isn't just hazardous to your health, it's hazardous to your image as a leader. Smoking is "out." It is no longer compatible with people's perception of an effective leader. If you smoke and want to be seen as a leader, become a closet smoker or snuff out the habit altogether.

17. *Facial expressions.* People recognize you by your face and tend to think that it tells them who you are. If you have a sad face, a worried face, a tense face, a frowning face, or a glowering face, they think that's the kind of person you are. Put the best face possible on your image. Look like what you are—a leader.

18. *Personal space.* Leaders want to get close to people, but not too close. It pays to respect other people's space. Most adults feel uncomfortable if strangers or anyone besides family and close friends invade their space (a zone of approximately 2 to 3 feet in each direction). Sensitive leaders don't touch or crowd those they don't know. People will respect you more if you respect their comfort zone.

19. *Coughing or sneezing.* Everyone has to cough or sneeze occasionally. How you do it, however, can make a big difference in the impression you make on others. It's not leaderlike to sneeze too loudly, cough in someone's face, or spray germs indiscriminately. Cover up. It's good for public health, and it's good for your image.

Voice Mail Etiquette and Profile for Leaders

- Keep recorded greetings and message requests simple and straight-forward. Avoid gimmicks.

- Check messages regularly—at least twice daily.

- Always listen to all of your messages. Don't skip old messages or ones from callers you'd prefer to avoid. You don't want to miss any important information.

- Respond to messages in a timely manner. (Many schools set 24 hours as the standard for acceptable response time.)

- Be organized. A rambling message may confuse the receiver.

- Speak naturally. Don't shout. The voice mail system isn't deaf.

- Identify yourself and who you are intending to leave a message for up front to avoid any possible mix-up or confusion.

- Don't use voice mail to duck direct contact with another party.

- Don't play games or try to be cute. "Guess who?" is for parties, not for conducting business.

- Don't use up too much recording time with small talk. Remember, this is a recorded message, not a social conversation.

- Don't leave frivolous, extraneous, or unnecessary messages.

- Avoid run-on messages.

- Remember that voice mail is no place for profanity or obscenities.

- Don't use voice mail to spread gossip or rumors.

- Don't say anything over voice mail that you wouldn't say in person.

- Make it easy for the receiver to respond. Indicate when you will be available for follow-up.

- Indicate what type of response is anticipated or desired.

20. *Wrinkled clothing.* Wrinkled clothes are as damaging to your image as dirty, ill-fitting, or outdated clothing. Wrinkles suggest sloppiness or lack of pride. Well-pressed clothing, however, looks sharp and creates a sharp image. That's the look of a leader.

Paying attention to all of the little details that determine how you come across to other people isn't being picky or phony; it's simply being your best. In image building, as in many aspect of leadership, if you take care of all of the little things, the big things will take care of themselves.

You may not be able to control your genes, age, native intelligence, or many aspects of your physical appearance, but you can largely control your image. If you want to look and act like an effective leader, you probably can. And if you do, you just may find that you have become one.

10

*Using the Tools
of Leadership*

Every occupation or profession has its own unique set of tools, and leadership is no different. What is different about leadership is that the tools tend to be the same no matter in what field the leader works. Because leaders work through other people, their tools are people tools—committees, teams, meetings, memos, reports, presentations, seminars, speeches, demonstrations, face-to-face encounters, correspondence, and so on.

These all seem very ordinary, but in the right hands, they are the tools that build dreams, visions, and victories in schools, businesses, governments, and organizations of all kinds.

Every rookie administrator and burned-out bureaucrat uses the same tools as the most successful leaders in the field. The difference is in how they use them.

Keep-the-lid-on managers use the traditional tools of leadership in standard, predictable ways, just as they've always used them (SS, DD— same stuff, different day). Impact leaders, on the other hand, use these same tools creatively, effectively, and differently for different purposes. In which camp would you rather be?

Anyone can write a memo. Not everyone, however, can write a memo that motivates readers, triggers action, and gets results. Not everyone who holds a hammer is a skilled carpenter. Not everyone who holds a meeting is a true leader. Masters of their crafts in all fields use common tools in uncommon ways.

If you want to learn how to use the tools of leadership like the most effective principals and superintendents, then this chapter's for you. Here's how the best leaders get better results from the same tools of the trade that their less effective counterparts use every day with little or limited success.

SPEAKING AND WRITING LIKE A LEADER

Leaders (not necessarily everyone who holds an administrative post, but true leaders) are communicators first and foremost. Words are their stock in trade. They don't spend all their time reading, writing, and speaking, but it often seems as if they do. History records that Napoleon wrote approximately 50,000 letters in his lifetime. That sounds like an average week to many principals and superintendents.

It's no accident that speaking and writing are the essential tools of leadership. Words—spoken and written—are powerful. They can inform, instruct, inspire, and evoke emotions. They shouldn't be squandered or used dishonestly. All good leaders know this. (School leaders should know it even better than others.) That's why effective leaders always try to use their words sparingly and well.

Unfortunately, many school administrators and managers in other fields are uncomfortable with words. They don't like to write, talk to people they don't know, or speak before a crowd. They don't think they're good at these activities. Sometimes, they even think they can get by without doing them. They might not realize it, but their reluctance and reticence just may be what is preventing them from bridging the gap between managing and truly leading. If you're one of these, get real. Speaking and writing are the tools that go with the territory. You can't do the job unless you use the right tools.

Occasionally, some would-be leaders also believe that if they can speak reasonably well, they don't have to worry about writing. Others think just the opposite. They're both wrong.

Although more and more school business is conducted in person, through small-group interaction, or over the phone, oral communication hasn't replaced the written word. Likewise, word processors, fax machines, e-mail, and copy machines haven't eliminated the need for effective verbal communication. Both speaking and writing are still equally crucial to effective leadership.

This doesn't mean, however, that all leaders have to be gifted writers or polished public speakers. They don't; but they do have to be able to communicate well enough to get the job done and to find ways to make words work for them.

If you're not particularly good at writing or speaking, don't do it any more than you have to. There are other means to tap into the power of words and to send strong messages without doing it all yourself. Don't be afraid to get a good ghostwriter or speechwriter or to have a talented assistant make many of the speeches (based on your input, of course). Good principals and superintendents do it all the time. It's better than embarrassing yourself needlessly or completely blowing your image as a leader.

Of course, there are times when the leader has to do the communicating directly. Sometimes substitutes won't do, and there just isn't any way to weasel out of it. At these times, if you want to lead, you have to be able to speak and write with acceptable clarity, accuracy, and effectiveness. These are standards that most people can achieve if they are willing to try, learn, work, and stretch themselves a bit. If this sounds like you, there's hope.

If you're not good at speaking or writing or both, you can get better. Everybody can. Practice helps. So does following the suggestions from professional speech and writing instructors outlined below. These 15 guidelines can help you speak and write like an effective leader, but they only work if you actually apply them.

1. Do your writing and public speaking only when there's a real reason for doing so, not just to prove that you're busy, important, or powerful.

2. Speak and write with a purpose and to a person(s). Have a goal and an audience in mind.

3. Think before you write anything (even a personal note) or prepare a speech (even short, informal greetings or welcoming comments). Don't just wade in counting on a sudden spontaneous burst of inspiration. (Inspiration is rarely sudden or spontaneous.)

It's not easy to write or speak simply and plainly. It takes hard work to make something sound effortless or read easily. Most good writers are plodders who carefully think their message through before they start throwing words at it.

4. Do your homework. Know your material and know your audience before you start writing or preparing a speech.

5. In both writing and public speaking, the same basic rules apply: Shorter is better, small words are better than big ones, and straight talk is the best talk.

Use as few words as possible. Keep your message simple and direct. Resist the temptation or impulse to become overly elegant. Just because you know a lot of fancy words does not mean that you have an obligation to use them.

6. Try to speak naturally (conversationally) and to write the way you speak.

7. Think about the tone of your message. Is it patronizing? Insulting? Does it sound arrogant or bossy? Is it whiny? Is it threatening or intimidating?

8. In both speaking and writing, take a tip from journalists and get to the point quickly. Put all the essential stuff up front. You never know how soon you may start losing the listener or reader.

9. Insist on zero tolerance for errors in written work. Make friends with a good spell-checking computer program. Have someone else proofread your work. (You can never properly proof your own material, because

How to Make Better Speeches and Presentations

- Know as much about you audience as possible. Who are they? Where do they come from? What is their background? Why are they here? How much do they know? What do they care about? What are their biases?

- Don't just practice your presentation—stage a full-blown dress rehearsal.

- Always have an outline and/or notes to fall back on in case your memory takes a vacation at the wrong time.

- Check out the physical amenities (i.e., lights, sound system, audiovisual equipment, water glass, etc.) in advance. Know where the switches are and how to get help if you need it.

- Never underestimate the importance of a great beginning. Get off to a fast start by identifying why you are making this speech at this time, what you hope to accomplish, and the main point of your talk as quickly as possible. Try to establish a bond with the listeners and start the audience thinking within the first 2 minutes.

- Keep your presentation short (no more than 20 minutes, if possible) and simple. Keep key points to a minimum.

- Be as relaxed and conversational as you can.

- Vary your speech rate and tone to maintain audience attention.

- Don't just stand there. Use gestures to support your words. Use props and audiovisual aids. Hold up something. Move around. Do something to show you're alive and more than just a talking head. It helps to hold audience interest and make you more relaxed as well.

- Be enthusiastic. If you can't get excited about your topic, why should anyone else?

- Be leery of humor. Jokes can backfire or fall flat. If you're not good at humor, don't feel obligated to use it.

- Stay focused throughout the entire speech. Know what you're talking about and why at every moment.

- Bring your presentation to closure. Summarize. End on a high note.

- When answering questions after a speech, always repeat each question; clarify the question if necessary; keep responses focused; handle each question quickly, honestly, and warmly; don't try to bluff; and don't drag out your answers.

you invariably tend to read what is supposed to be in the text, not what it actually says.)

Every writer needs an editor. A good secretary can fill the bill. There's nothing more damaging or embarrassing than a memo, letter, or report from a school leader that contains glaring punctuation, grammatical, or spelling errors. Don't let it happen on your watch.

10. Don't ramble (on paper or out loud). Cut out extraneous words. Avoid gobbledygook and jargon—especially jargon. For example, no subject

is more clouded by unrecognizable educational jargon than school finance. School funding is inherently complex and confusing. Few administrators fully understand it. Laypeople don't have a clue. They need and expect straight talk, clear-cut explanations, and understandable illustrations and interpretations from the professionals. Instead, they routinely get jibberish in the form of a specialized language of highly legal and technical terms such as: equalized levy, excess levy referendum, tax increment financing, and weighted average daily membership (WADM).

11. Never read or memorize a speech. Nothing causes an audience's eyes to glaze over faster than a "canned" presentation.

12. Feel free to use form letters or to borrow from books of sample letters, memos, and speeches for educators if you need to. They often can help you put together a better letter, memo, or speech than you could write yourself.

13. Don't hesitate to call on the district communications or public relations specialist for help with your communications in general or with a specific item or project. That's what they're there for.

14. Try to make eye contact, even when speaking to large groups. It helps to hold the audience and make you feel more at ease.

15. Take time to outline and/or make a rough draft of all written work. It's like practicing a speech in front of a mirror. Both are essential.

These general pointers are second nature to most accomplished leaders. They can be for you, too, if you work on them. For more help with

Steps to Successful Writing

Every formal writing task deserves to be done right. Here are the steps many pros follow. They just may work for you too.

- **Plan**—Let the message incubate for a while before doing any actual writing. Think about it. Let your subconscious process it.

- **Outline**—Don't skip this step. You need a blueprint to build a solid piece of written communication.

- **Rough Draft**—No one (not even a seasoned writer) is perfect the first time.

- **Cooling-Off Period**—Take time to regain your objectivity.

- **Rewrite**—Prepare final draft.

- **Proofread**—At least twice!

- **Polish**—Add any finishing touches.

- **Celebrate**—Reward yourself.

Tips for Better Letter Writing

- Write in an informal style.

- Keep the format logical.

- Get to the point quickly.

- Keep the tone of the letter professional, friendly, and upbeat (if possible).

- Omit irrelevant information.

- Strive to be nonjudgmental.

- Stick to monosyllabic words as much as possible.

- Avoid acronyms or confusing technical terms.

- Limit letters to one page whenever possible.

- End on an encouraging note as often as you can.

Tips for Writing Memos That Get Read and Get Results

Even the much maligned memo can be a powerful communication tool if used properly. Here's how:

- Never write a memo when you have nothing worthwhile to say or when another communication tool will work better.

- Remember: Short memos get read. All others get skimmed, filed, or tossed.

- Memos are best used to clarify goals or issues, present new information, make recommendations, define responsibilities, pinpoint accountability, settle disputes, go on record, present arguments, or persuade readers.

- The best memos stand alone and take the place of a needless meeting.

- Make sure that readers learn something from your memos. Otherwise, they're just exercises.

- Make your memos clear and understandable.

- Make the purpose of the memo clear at the beginning.

- Make clear what is expected of the reader.

- Try to make each memo complete enough to minimize or preclude follow-up questions.

- If appropriate, include a deadline for responding.

specific areas of speaking and writing common to school leaders, use the breakout tips below.

Speaking and writing are powerful tools for leaders at all levels, but they can lose their power if they are abused or overused.

Tips for Better Report Writing

The following suggestions and precautions will help produce better written reports:

- Accumulate data as quickly as possible. Reports should be completed in a timely manner or not at all.
- Take time in selecting a title.
- Don't use a fancy type or font style.
- Strive for an attention-grabbing first paragraph.
- Personalize the writing as much as possible.
- Use plain words.
- Don't overuse slang, jargon, or technical talk.
- Avoid acronyms and abbreviations.
- Watch out for sexist terms.
- Simplify data and omit all irrelevant statistics.
- Avoid clichés.
- Don't include anything that will only confuse the reader.
- Put backup and supporting details in appendixes.
- Proofread carefully. (Reading out loud helps.)

Always strive to improve your communication skills if you want to grow as a leader. They will get better with practice. That's a guarantee!

But no matter how good you get, remember that leaders can talk or write too much. People quit paying attention after a while. Sensitive leaders don't anesthetize their audience with communication overload.

Part of effective speaking and writing is knowing when to shut up or sign off. Silence can be an effective tool of leadership too.

HOW TO MAKE MEETINGS WORK FOR YOU

Educators must love meetings—they have so many of them. Although numerous surveys show that upper-level managers in business and industry spend 60% to 70% of their time in meetings, the percentage must be even higher for many principals and superintendents.

Because of the great frequency and variety of meetings they attend, an outsider might think that school personnel enjoy meetings and find them profitable and productive. Wrong! Most ordinary administrators (and other staff members) detest meetings. They think that the vast majority are boring wastes of time. Nevertheless, they can't break the meeting habit.

Effective leaders, however, aren't in the habit of holding meetings that waste time. They use meetings as a tool of leadership only when they are needed, when they are the best vehicle for reaching specific ends, and when they are most likely to produce results. Good leaders have a lot of meetings, but they know how to make their meetings work for them.

The first step is to know when to call a meeting and when not to. There are certain kinds of meetings that should never happen because they are purposeless and perfunctory. These are the ones that give good meetings a bad name. Nothing turns people off faster than a worthless meeting that leads the participants nowhere.

Many principals and superintendents hold meetings just because they're on the calendar. Some have regularly scheduled meetings whether they need them or not. ("We've always met on Monday morning.") There's no use having a weekly or monthly meeting if there's no real reason for it. Good leaders don't call a meeting just for the sake of having a meeting.

Some meetings should be a memo. If the only reason for calling people together is to disseminate information, a well-written memorandum will achieve the same goal more quickly and easily without generating a lot of grumbling from captive audience members.

Meetings work only when they are clearly the most effective way to achieve a worthwhile goal. Successful leaders don't call meetings that should never happen, such as the following:

- Meetings called on short notice so that no one has time to prepare
- Meetings called during a particularly busy or inconvenient time for school personnel
- Meetings in which participants are asked to make decisions without sufficient background information
- Meetings that deal with old news
- Meetings called when too many key people can't attend
- Meetings that are premature

The best meetings are brief, focused, and productive. If you want to make the most of faculty, staff, or other meetings, ask these questions before scheduling them: (a) Is this the best way to use everyone's time? (b) Is there a better way to accomplish the same thing? (c) Is the timing right? (d) Who needs to be there? and (e) Is there enough advance notice so that people can properly prepare?

Even when it's the right meeting for the right reason at the right time, it still may not work. A meeting that bombs is worse than no meeting because it leaves everyone disappointed and disgruntled. There are lots of reasons why a potentially successful meeting may go wrong. Usually, the problems could have been avoided or corrected in advance. Meetings are most likely to fall flat for one or more of the following causes:

- The group is too large.
- The wrong people attend (or the right people don't).
- The agenda is too long.
- The meeting is unstructured and allowed to drift.
- The outcome is predetermined.
- Communication goes only one way.
- The meeting deals with superficial issues (not real ones).
- There are too many surprises.
- The meeting has a hidden agenda.
- Nothing is decided or accomplished.

Managers just call meetings and wait to see what happens. Real leaders set up their meetings for success by eliminating the potential pitfalls above. The best way to escape meeting mishaps and guarantee success is to have a well-organized, manageable agenda.

Good meetings start with a good agenda. The agenda is like a "promo" for a movie. It sets the tone and lets people know what to expect. A well-developed agenda serves as an outline that guides the direction of the meeting. The order of items sends a message about priorities and signals what's most important to the organization.

If an agenda looks interesting and worthwhile, people look forward to attending. If it looks like a legal brief, the meeting is dead in the water before it ever starts. If it's too vague, people will wonder why they should attend and will start looking for excuses to skip it. It always helps to involve stakeholders in developing an agenda. (After all, it's their meeting, too.)

When a meeting is appropriately timed and structured by a focused agenda, it should work. Just to make sure, however, successful leaders pay attention to all of the little details that can derail even a well-planned meeting. Experienced meeting conveners offer these tips to make every meeting work for you:

- Have a well-defined purpose that is clear to the participants. Use meetings to solve problems, not just as a bulletin board for announcements.

- Select a convenient date. (Avoid scheduling meetings too early or too late in the day—especially late on Friday afternoon.)

- Send out advance agendas. Include a beginning and ending time on the agenda.

- If you want to conduct a meeting like a leader, sit where a leader sits. Take the "power perch" at the head or in the center of the table.

- Arrange seating so that all participants can see one another.

- Start and end on time. Make it a tradition.

- Lead, rather than run, the meeting. Be a facilitator, not a lecturer.

• Don't let any one person (including yourself) dominate the discussion. Participation is the key to productive meetings.

• Be careful about who records the minutes. (Some leaders take their own minutes of the meeting even while conducting it. It's not as hard or as crazy as it sounds.) When the meeting becomes history and memories fade, the only proof of what happened is the minutes. Who prepares the minutes determines and controls the truth later.

• Pace the meeting. Watch the clock. Keep things moving. Some successful leaders even put time limits on each agenda item.

• Lighten up. Don't take the meeting or yourself too seriously.

• Encourage open and honest dialogue.

• Be flexible. Allow for detours and unexpected directions.

• Invite humor to attend any meeting you conduct.

• Recap what was discussed and agreed upon. Define next steps.

• Always include something upbeat, and try to end every meeting on a positive note.

Effective leaders use meetings as a legitimate tool of leadership by controlling their number, frequency, and length, and by paying attention to all of the essential details of planning and conducting them. They also do one more thing that many average administrators fail to do—they listen!

One of the best ways to make meetings work for you is to practice active listening. Listen to what is really being said. Listen between the lines to the emotions, attitudes, and feelings beyond the words. A meeting can be an accurate barometer for measuring the pressure within the group if you concentrate enough to read it.

Listening Tips for Leaders

• Be interested in what others say.

• Listen nonjudgmentally.

• Be comfortable with silence.

• Paraphrase. Ask clarifying questions.

• Check to see if nonverbal messages match verbal ones.

• Ask "why" questions.

• Pay attention to what is not said.

• Avoid interrupting or jumping to conclusions.

Even though everyone complains about them, meetings are only as good or as bad as the people who run them and participate in them. Mediocre managers have mediocre meetings. Effective leaders have effective meetings. They use meetings as a practical tool to get things done, not just as a means of occupying people's time.

If you want to know how you're doing as a leader, look at the meetings you conduct. Are they productive? Worthwhile? Interesting? Well attended? If not, you haven't passed the litmus test of leadership yet. It's time to improve your meetings or to start canceling a lot of them in a hurry.

Good meetings are important for achieving organizational goals. They also help to define your leadership image. How you present yourself and the impression you convey at meetings affects how others see you as a leader.

GUIDELINES FOR WORKING WITH COMMITTEES

As stated earlier, by definition, leaders work through other people. Obviously, it's too awkward and time consuming to randomly reach out to others to assist in attaining organizational goals. There has to be a more structured, organized, and efficient way to do it. That's why we have committees. All organizations have them, but schools have more than most.

Committees are the way that schools and school systems do business. When they work, committees help gather data, identify options, evaluate choices, and recommend action.

Of course, not all committees do work. Some are nonproductive. Some are mostly a diversion. Some do more harm than good. Nevertheless, committees are here to stay, and leaders have to learn to use them to their advantage.

Even though many managers don't like committees (mostly because they don't know how to use them), good committees do get things done and can make a difference.

Committees are tools. They can be mishandled. Used properly, however, they can be a leader's best friend and good right arm. Committees are still the best way a leader has to get results using other people's skills, talents, imagination, inspiration, energy, and know-how.

Sometimes, it may be difficult to live and work with so many committees. It would be even harder, though, to live, work, and lead without them.

Like many tools, committees don't come with an instruction manual. The best way to learn to use them effectively is to find out how the best principals and superintendents do it. You might be surprised how easy it is to turn a ho-hum committee into a humdinger action group.

Even if you've had nightmarish experiences with committees that did more bickering than business, didn't know what they were supposed to do or how to do it, and ended up accomplishing nothing, don't give up. Remember, it's up to leaders to see to it that committees deliver on their promises, live up to their potential, and fulfill their purpose. That's why they get to be called leaders. If you want to claim the name, play the game like they do.

The following guidelines can help you get more out of your committees starting immediately. These are the measures that leading administrators take to ensure committee success:

- Define the areas of responsibility. Be sure everyone understands the scope of the committee's work.
- Limit the focus. Explain clearly what outcome or product is expected of the committee.
- Set time limits and target dates.
- Remember that committees are only as good as the people who serve on them. Choose members carefully. (It's hard to get rid of a troublesome member once the committee is operational.) Strive for a mix of expertise, background, perspectives, and viewpoints. Include a balance of males, females, minorities, professionals, community members, and students (where appropriate). One of the biggest mistakes that many administrators make is not including students on committees that deal with student issues.
- Limit membership to a manageable size. (Anything over a dozen is usually too large.)
- Set term limits for ongoing committees.
- Provide adequate resources, clerical support, materials, and background information.
- Arrange for necessary record keeping and reporting.
- Establish ground rules as necessary, and keep them simple.
- Provide a suitable environment for committee work.
- Guard against lay members being intimidated by the professionals on the committee.
- Start with a process for enabling members to get to know each other.
- Set meeting times for the convenience of the members, not the leader.
- Allow each committee to elect its own officers.
- Make it clear that all members can suggest agenda topics.
- Require periodic progress reports. Don't allow any committee to disappear between the cracks.
- Remember that committees, like athletic teams, need occasional pep talks.
- Once a committee is pointed in the right direction, get out of the way.
- Accept and validate all committee reports or recommendations. Do something with whatever a committee comes up with. Don't let members feel that they have been used as pawns, or that their work has been only window dressing.

Effective leaders accept that committees are inevitable, are an integral part of the school's communication and decision-making system, and serve as important links with the community. If you don't learn how to get results from committee work, you've lost control of an important instrument for successful leadership.

MANAGING WHILE WALKING AROUND (MWWA): LEADERSHIP UP CLOSE AND PERSONAL

Management while walking around (MWWA) is a popular leadership tool in today's corporate world. The most respected CEOs don't spend much time in the boardroom or the executive suite. They make it a point to be out and about, maintaining close contact with employees and customers alike.

They don't just read about company gains and losses—they see and hear firsthand what's working and what's not. They know the people in the organization who make things happen, and these people know them. In the business community, isolation is no longer an acceptable management style—if it ever was.

It should come as no surprise that effective school leaders have always known this. Good principals and superintendents don't lead from behind a desk or at the other end of the intercom. They go where the action is.

Some administrators like to spend time behind their desk—in their office—with the door closed. They build buffers and barriers to insulate themselves. That's why they will always be managers rather than leaders.

Other principals and superintendents spend as much time as possible being visible, available, and accessible. They stay in touch with students and staff and with what is *really* going on in the organization. They understand that face-to-face feedback, support, clarification, and reinforcement are prerequisites to achieving the dream of the organization. They practice MWWA on a daily basis. They are the true leaders.

If you have your eye on the winner's circle for leaders, don't grow too fond of your office. The best leadership is always up close and personal.

Unfortunately, being visible isn't easy. It requires time and extra effort and means saying no to lots of other appealing tasks and activities that can get between the leader and the real world of the school.

MWWA is what all administrators say they want to do, but many are too busy. Real leaders, on the other hand, don't say much about it, they just do it. Even the busiest leaders find ways to practice MWWA. It's too good a leadership tool on which to miss out.

If you ever want a quick check on the quality of leadership in any school, just ask the students if they know who the principal is. Where the chief administrator is more than a voice over the public address system and most kids know his or her name, you can be pretty sure that there's a real leader in charge. Chalk it up to MWWA. It's a leadership tool you can't do without.

Tips for Better One-on-One Conferencing and Coaching

- Use the other party's name to help personalize the conference.

- Have a purpose in mind.

- Listen carefully. Don't interrupt the other party.

- Use questions to narrow the focus.

- Be sincere (authentic). Maintain a pleasant tone to the extent possible.

- Actively involve the other party.

- Use notes if necessary.

- Slow down. Rushing things is never a good conference technique.

- Respect confidentiality.

- Honor (respect) the other party's views, positions, responses, and contributions.

- Use positive examples whenever possible.

- Be honest. Don't soft-pedal bad news.

- Teach rather than preach. Apply the principles of learning.

- Don't try to include too much in a single session.

- Use closure techniques.

- Remain professional

- Have fun (as appropriate).

DON'T OVERLOOK THESE OTHER LEADERSHIP TOOLS

No matter how good a leader you are, you can't create a solid, successful organization solely on the power of your personality or the sheer force of your will. You also have to use the right tools. Even great mechanics need the proper tools to keep an engine running smoothly. The same principle applies to keeping an organization running at optimum capacity and efficiency.

That's why most leaders are picky about their tools. They choose to use only what works (i.e., what works for them, not necessarily for anyone else).

Speaking, writing, meetings, committees, and MWWA are all tools that most effective school leaders use every day. Even past history (including founders' tales, folk heroes, organizational legends, and historical precedents) can be instruments of leadership. If you can use these tools well, you'll become an effective leader. If you mishandle them, you may have to struggle to achieve even average success.

Naturally, there's more to it than this. There are many tools at the disposal of resourceful leaders. A tool can be anything that may be used or applied to make things work better and to move the organization closer to its vision.

Some things may not be recognized easily as possible leadership tools, but if they do the job, they qualify. If you have what it takes to become a leader, you probably can think of lots of other tools that may help achieve desired goals. If you do, don't hesitate to use them.

At the same time, don't overlook the following 10 common instruments that, in the right hands, can help perform leadership miracles:

1. *Data.* Information is power, but data are just data. They can be either revealing or misleading. Leaders need data that are accessible, reliable, accurate, and easily understood to use as the basis for planning and problem solving. Bad data can lead only to bad decisions. Insist on the best, most up-to-date information. It's a leader's way.

2. *Budgets.* How money is allocated and spent within the organization sends a strong message about what's important. Budgets should reflect priorities. Limited revenue requires that important things get funded and things that are mostly diversions or distractions don't. Good leaders put their money where their mouths are.

3. *Calendars.* How things are spaced and placed throughout the year indicate their importance and influence the likelihood that they will receive maximum attention. The calendar is a tool that savvy leaders use to ensure that important things happen on time at the right time and to the advantage of the organization.

4. *Time.* Most managers don't think of time as a tool, but effective leaders do. Whatever gets the most time gets done. The best principals and superintendents see to it that prime matters receive prime time. Time shouldn't just happen. It should be used as a tool of leadership.

5. *Technology.* This is *the* leadership tool of the 21st century. Any leader who doesn't take maximum advantage of today's and tomorrow's technology is a fool. Leaders don't have to know everything about how to use all of the latest technologies, but they should know what is available, what it will do, and how to access it.

If you don't have a couple of computer wizards on your staff, you're unfairly handicapping your own leadership capability and your school's chances for long-term success.

6. *Contacts.* Professionals make contacts for a reason. A network of contacts is a rich source of support, advice, and assistance. The more contacts you have, the more resources you have. This is another good reason for active participation in professional organizations at the state and national level.

Most administrators think of their contacts merely as cronies and fellow sufferers. Astute leaders see them as possible consultants and sounding boards. Your contacts are part of your repertoire of leadership tools. Don't be afraid to use them.

7. *Authority.* The authority of your position as an administrator carries with it a certain limited amount of power that can be used as a tool of leadership. It's a fragile power, however, that can backfire if misused.

Good leaders don't use their authority to get a preferred parking spot, but they do use it to enforce decisions, break deadlocks, weigh in on important issues, and set a tone. The right thing to do is to scrupulously avoid abusing authority while never hesitating to use it for the greater good of the organization.

8. *The media.* Most administrators feel used by the media. In truth, skillful leaders can use the media as well (see Chapter 7 for suggestions). Media reps can be educated, informed, influenced, persuaded, convinced, baited, enticed, and even led to a limited extent. Smart leaders don't try to manipulate the media, but they do use them as a tool to get the facts out and to shape public opinion where appropriate.

9. *Eyes and ears.* Most people have two eyes and two ears, but many don't really see or hear. (How many administrators do you know who go through life wearing blinders that prevent them from seeing trouble or problems-in-the-making?) Leaders don't just see and hear, they really observe and listen. They pay attention.

A leader's eyes and ears are often the best sources of firsthand knowledge about what's really going on. They can be effective tools of leadership if they stay attuned, focused, and open to reality.

10. *People.* The most critical and important tools that any leaders possess are the people who work for and with them. Staff members, assistants, and aides are all extensions of the leader. All leaders rise and fall on the backs of others. That's why it always pays to hire the best. Hire better than yourself.

Nurture talent in others, and give it opportunities to show itself. Remarkable leaders in all fields specialize in "growing talent." This means more than merely recruiting and hiring good people. It involves nurturing potential, providing opportunities (including training), challenging, coaching, encouraging, delegating responsibilities, trusting, taking a risk, opening up career and advancement possibilities, grooming future educational leaders, and being willing to promote from within. If you want to shine as a leader, surround yourself with bright people and let them make you look good.

This list of potential leadership tools could go on and on. All good leaders are constantly searching for new tools and new uses for old tools and techniques to help them become more effective. If you want to survive as a leader, you'll do the same.

Keep your eyes open for anything that can help you get the job done better, faster, or more easily. Try to recognize the hidden power in the ordinary. A leader's tools are whatever works.

Artisans and craftspeople in all fields are only as good as the tools they use and their skill at using them. It's true for the art of leadership as well. If you master use of the essential tools of leadership, you can't stop yourself from becoming a more effective leader.

Some of the best advice you'll ever get is to check your toolkit often to be sure it's up to date and keep practicing to improve your use of all of the leadership tools at your command. Leaders lead only as long as they keep getting better. After that, they're just coasting.

11

Communication Tips for School Leaders

L eadership and communication are synonymous. If you can't communicate adequately, you can't lead. It's that simple. Of all the essential tools of leadership, communication skills are the most important by far.

Some dead-end managers may be able to get by with holing up, shuffling paper, dodging issues, giving vague answers, remaining noncommittal, and avoiding as much forthright communication as possible. Leaders can't.

No matter whether they work in the public or the private sector, leaders have to communicate openly, honestly, and often. They understand that words are the lifeblood of leadership. They know that people who are afraid of words are usually afraid of ideas as well.

Again, this doesn't mean that all leaders have to be poet laureates, oracles, or orators. Being able to express ideas clearly and with feeling is all that's required.

High schools and colleges everywhere offer courses in speaking and writing because they know that ordinary people can learn to improve their communication skills. It happens every day. If you want to prepare for leadership, this should be your first step.

UNDERSTANDING THE ELEMENTS OF SCHOOL COMMUNICATION

Solid communication is at the core of every successful organization. Each organization, however, has its own unique needs and nuances for channeling information.

Schools, in particular, have a singular culture that calls for specialized approaches to internal and external communication. That's why efforts to transplant business executives or lawyers into school administrative posts don't always work. Sometimes, their communication (leadership) styles don't fit the traditions and mores of the school community.

Unlike many organizations, communication is what schools and education are all about. The school leader has primary responsibility for ensuring an effective flow of communication throughout the organization and between the school and its multiple audiences.

Unfortunately, some administrators fail to realize that they are constantly communicating. Every action by a school official sends a message that has the potential for being misread, misunderstood, misconstrued, or misinterpreted.

Effective leaders realize that they have a special communication obligation because everyone in town wants to know about the schools. This makes every message from the top a form of public relations.

That's why communication is too important to leave to chance. Good leaders don't let internal or external communication just happen. To be effective, communication needs to be carefully planned, systematically managed, and continuously monitored and refined. It starts by understanding that communication isn't just about sending messages. It's also about receiving information and giving feedback. Communication within the organization and with those outside works only when it's a two-way flow. As chief communicator, the leader must consider not only the content to be conveyed but also the capacity of the intended audience to receive it and the likelihood that it will be understood. The goal is always to transfer ideas or information from the source to an intended audience essentially *unchanged* (what is heard is actually more important than what is said). In every communication situation, the key questions that leaders need to ask and answer are the following:

1. What do you want to communicate?

2. Why do you want to communicate this message?

3. Who needs to get the message?

4. How should the message be communicated?

5. When is the best time to communicate it?

A sound school communication loop looks like this:

Figure 11.1   The Good Communication Cycle

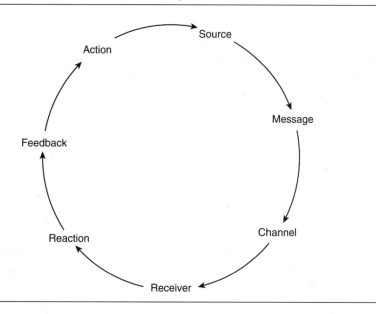

The tricky part of communication is that it can break down at any point in the cycle. All of the elements have to be in place and properly addressed to ensure adequate and accurate understanding. One of the first rules of good communication is to get the attention of the intended receiver. This requires knowing who your exact audience is and how to reach it. Few leaders are called on to interact with as many audiences as school principals and superintendents are. At various times, school leaders communicate specifically with dozens of separate and distinct groups, and not all forms of communication work equally well with all of these audiences. Communication doesn't come in "one size fits all." For example, the licensed staff may readily understand the jargon of the profession, but senior citizens may not. Likewise, community business leaders may be able to grasp and interpret statistical financial data that are incomprehensible to many parents. Some audiences will read published material from the school, and some will not. Some groups are readily accessible, whereas others are hard to reach. A solid school communication plan takes into account all of these audiences and factors. Each of the school's diverse publics has distinct interests, needs, and agendas. Each, at least sometimes, must be targeted separately.

It helps to keep the specific audience in mind each time you plan a communication strategy. One technique that many leaders use is to visualize the targeted individual or group each time they draft a memo, prepare a speech, or edit a newsletter. It's also wise to test communications on representatives of the targeted population before going public. When customizing communications for a specific audience, it pays to consider not just the content of the message but also the format, medium, delivery, and

Tips on Targeting Communications for Senior Citizens

When trying to reach older audiences, here's what works best:

- Think of your audience as active and informed, not old.
- Use humor, but not at their expense. Don't depict seniors as sappy, bumbling, or ineffectual.
- Don't patronize. (Talking down to older people is like talking louder to the blind. Seniors are just old, not simple.)
- Avoid the term *elderly*. (It comes across as meaning "decrepit.")
- Be upbeat. Be honest. Be brief!

timing. One of the secrets of successful school communications is to not have any secrets. Be open. Avoid transparent euphemisms. Tell it like it is. Inform everyone who has a need to know.

Withholding information is seldom a successful strategy for any leader. Other important communication lessons that many leaders have learned the hard way include the following:

- Always plan to use multiple delivery channels. Never assume that one attempt at communicating will be sufficient. Plan to convey important messages several times in several different ways. Repeated material is only boring to those who paid attention the first time. To everyone else, it's new information.
- Avoid information overload. (There's no reason to tell people a lot more than they want to know.)
- Use technical terms sparingly, if at all.
- Be sensitive to cultural differences.
- Acknowledge other viewpoints when appropriate.
- Avoid any argumentative or combative statements as much as possible.
- Omit emotional or loaded language that might heighten any existing disagreements.
- Resist the urge to be sarcastic.

Communication isn't someone else's business. It's every leader's basic responsibility. That's true in all organizations, but it's especially true in schools. As indicated earlier, to become a better leader, work on becoming a better communicator. It's not that hard. The following additional tips can help get you started.

MORE WRITING TIPS FOR SCHOOL LEADERS

Written expression in one form or another is a cornerstone for effective communication. Writing is something that most administrators do every day. Unfortunately, some never get any better at it. It's their own fault, because they don't try. You can do better. If you really want to improve, dare to diagnose your own writing. Become your own worst critic. Put your ego aside and take a hard look at what you're doing right and what you're doing wrong.

Work as hard on evaluating your written work after you've finished it as you do writing it in the first place. The key to improvement is simply to know your weak spots and to work on them. It's always helpful to get critiques and feedback from others, but it's even better if you can objectively judge your own work, applaud yourself for your successes, recognize your flaws, and try to do better next time. Writing is a little like playing golf. It keeps you humble. The more you do it, the better you get, but, at the same time, the more you realize how much better you could be. Sometimes, you get it just right. Other times, you struggle to get it at all. Writing is powerful. It should be handled with care, but it shouldn't be feared. Writing can also be challenging, exciting, therapeutic, and even fun. Becoming a great writer is not going to happen for very many of us. To become good enough, however, is within almost everyone's grasp. What's hard about writing is that there's always room for improvement. There will always be a better way to say it. What's easy about writing is that the fundamentals are attainable. The only overriding rule for good writing is simply to write clearly.

Writing plainly isn't easy, but it's possible. Just put one word in front of another until the job is done. That's all there is to it. To be an effective leader, you're going to have to write. You might just as well learn to do it right. The insider tips that follow can help correct any deficiencies your self-diagnosis discloses.

- Never write a memo, letter, report, or speech when you're angry, scared, hurt, or fatigued.
- If it helps, have a special place to write. (It doesn't have to be in your office.) Sometimes, a special setting helps get you into the mood to write and makes the words flow easier.
- Don't rush into writing. Do the preliminaries (i.e., thinking, researching, and organizing). Prewriting is as important as rewriting. Many accomplished writers agree that 90% of writing is internal. The rest happens on the page.
- If you have a hard time getting started, try asking a question, using a quote, leading with an attention-getting fact, or issuing a challenge.
- Start general and end with specifics.
- Choose words carefully. Don't just write down the first word that pops into your head.
- Get a good grammar guide and use it when you need it.
- Don't clutter up your work with unnecessary words or phrases.
- Don't overuse word intensifiers such as *really*, *very*, and *totally*.
- Avoid fragments (incomplete sentences) and/or run-on sentences. (These errors are more common than most people realize.)

- Don't go overboard on detail. You're not being paid by the word.
- Try to limit sentences to 17 words or less.
- Don't start too many sentences with "There are. . . ."
- Begin sentences in different ways and vary sentence length.
- Use words that appeal to the five senses whenever possible.
- Substitute simple, conversational words for complicated ones.
- Break longer sentences into shorter ones.
- Take a cue from journalists and always try to answer who, what, when, where, and why.
- Don't skimp on rewriting. It's called polishing. Every good writer does it.
- Don't be afraid of writing. Limited writing skills won't keep you from becoming an effective leader unless you let them. Leaders are known for their persistence. It's that persistence that can help you learn to write well enough and then some. It can help improve your speaking skills as well.

MORE SPEAKING TIPS FOR SCHOOL LEADERS

Like good writing, effective public speaking and successful oral presentations are the result of practice and forethought. Many administrators would be amazed at how long and hard the leaders they admire for being able to speak effortlessly really work to appear spontaneous. It takes a lot of time and preparation just to speak off-the-cuff.

All leaders have occasions to speak formally and informally to both large and small groups. It's part of a leader's life. It's no different for a school leader. If that's what you want to be, you'd better get used to it and get prepared for it.

Most people who give enough speeches eventually get pretty good at it, and you can too. You can even speed up the process through practice and by observing how really effective speakers do it. You can't be them, but you can pick up enough tricks of the trade to help you develop your own style and become an adequate or better speaker in your own right.

When it comes to mastering basic public speaking skills, as in many aspects of leadership, the difference between those who succeed and those who don't is mostly a matter of will. If you put it off, it won't happen. If you make up your mind to do it, it will. It's that easy.

To make it even easier, below are further tips from top speakers that you can use the next time you have to face a group of any size:

- Prepare with both the topic and the listeners in mind. Tailor the subject matter and gear the vocabulary to each specific audience.
- Believe in your message. Give your own speech. Use your own words.
- Your goal should be to present a clear message using powerful word choices.

Speaker's Checklist

Before giving your next speech or presentation, check out the following:

_____ *Seating arrangement*. Are there enough chairs? Can you get close to the audience?

_____ *Acoustics*. Can everyone hear?

_____ *Sight lines*. Can everyone see?

_____ *Lighting*. Is it adequate? Can it be adjusted? Where is the dimmer switch?

_____ *Temperature*. Is it comfortable? How is it regulated? Where are the controls?

_____ *Podium*. Is it the right height? Does the podium light work? Is there a fresh glass of water on the podium?

_____ *Microphone*. Does it work? Is there a backup?

_____ *Audiovisual equipment*. Is it set up? Does it work? Are there extra bulbs and fuses? Is a technician available in case of emergency?

- Always number your note cards. Don't even think about stapling them together.
- When rehearsing, pay attention to timing. Resist the tendency to talk too fast. It's a mistake that many inexperienced speakers make.
- For best rehearsal results, videotape your practice sessions and review them for areas to improve.
- Personally check out the location and setting of each speech in advance.
- Make friends with your nervousness. Use the energy to become more animated in your presentation.
- Plan what to do with your hands. If nothing else, keep them at your side or rest one on the podium.
- Pay attention to posture. Maintain a professional demeanor. If you look like a leader, you're more likely to sound like one as well.
- Do whatever it takes to get the audience's attention early in the presentation.
- Stay clear of ethnic stories, risqué humor, and jokes that belittle others.
- Use visual aids wherever they fit. (Remember that 80% of what people remember, they pick up visually.)
- Don't be afraid to pause to let your message sink in. An occasional lower and slower tone can also focus the audience's attention.
- Always try to end with a clincher.

Following these tips can set you up for success any time you have to make a presentation. The rest is up to you.

Speaking and presenting skills are to a leader what fishing tackle is to an angler. They're essential tools of the trade. You'd better start stocking up.

Ultimately, the only way to learn how to make effective speeches and presentations is to make speeches and presentations. Stretch yourself. Be willing to be uncomfortable. Force yourself to talk to people you don't know. Volunteer to give short talks and make presentations to unfamiliar groups. Keep at it. You'll get better. The alternative is to just sit back, keep quiet, and let someone else take over as leader.

TIPS ON NONVERBAL COMMUNICATION

Sometimes, if you listen to everything that is said and make it a point to hear every word, you still miss half of the conversation. Gestures, body talk, and nonverbal messages make up a "silent language" that communicates as effectively as spoken language to those who know how to decode it. Learning to read the vocabulary of body language is a shortcut to "hearing" the real message behind the words.

Words can deceive, but the body rarely lies. People can regulate their words, but they usually can't control their blinking, breathing, or perspiring. Often, gestures speak louder than spoken words. That's why, when the spoken words don't match the body language, experienced communicators tend to believe the nonverbal message.

Most people—including most school administrators—aren't attuned to nonverbal language. They don't pay attention to it. They don't "speak" the language. They hardly know it exists.

Most successful leaders, on the other hand, understand that all individuals and groups send vital messages through their posture, gestures, and body movements, and that body language is a powerful and expressive medium. They're open to receiving nonverbal messages as well as verbal ones. That's why they often understand what's really going on in a group, meeting, or social situation, whereas others don't have a clue.

Picking up on nonverbal language is part of paying attention and being aware. That's one of the things effective leaders do best. We've all seen it at work.

For example, CEOs often have an edge in the boardroom and know when to call for a vote and when to delay because they grasp unspoken messages that everyone else misses. Likewise, the best school leaders frequently know when to push and when to back off because they can spot when the body language and the spoken language agree and when they don't. Skillful public speakers also use body language to sense a crowd's reaction and to know when to stop talking.

Leaders in all fields make it a point to read body language. They learn to do it the same way they learned to read the printed work—by observing, becoming familiar with the symbols, making connections, and practicing.

If you want to get to the top and stay on top, you can't afford to let body language remain a foreign language for long. Learn to listen with your eyes as well as your ears. The more you understand about nonverbal communication, the better position you are in to lead any group.

Gestures and other body messages can be either intuitive or acquired. In both instances, they almost always occur spontaneously and unconsciously. That's why it's hard for people to mask the messages their bodies send out.

Although all body parts can be used to send out nonverbal messages, the hands, face, mouth, and eyes are the most expressive communicators. Sometimes, the full body sends a signal or conveys an important message.

Nonverbal Message Centers

From where do nonverbal messages come? About anywhere on the body. Look for body language clues from all of these sources:

Head	Forehead	Mouth
Eye	Neck	Muscles
Eyebrows	Shoulders	Arms
Nose	Tongue	Hands
Lips	Spine	Feet

Within any given society or culture, body signals tend to be universal and consistent. That's why it's possible to learn to read unintentional nonverbal cues and clues. Here are some of the most common body messages to watch for:

- Touching the nose, rubbing the eyes, or excessive blinking often conveys lying or fear of getting caught.
- Leaning forward indicates interest. Leaning away or turning to the side usually conveys just the opposite.
- Frequently adjusting the collar or other clothing indicates discomfort.
- Legs crossed at the ankles often sends a message of insecurity.
- Open arms and open hands frequently indicates an openness to listening and paying attention to another person.
- A lowered head or lowered eyes suggest inapproachability.

Being aware of these signals helps leaders to accurately interpret what others are really feeling and saying and to learn how to speak more effectively with their own bodies as well.

Principals and superintendents are highly visible public officials. From small conferences to large convocations, they are in the public eye. Their image often becomes the school's image in many people's minds. This is another reason to pay attention to body language—your own and everyone else's.

Nonverbal messages are an important part of human communication. You can't ignore them and expect to keep up with other leaders. Sometimes, you have to close your eyes to hear the speaker's words clearly; but other times, you have to open your eyes to get the full message.

YOU CAN'T KILL THE GRAPEVINE

There are a lot of administrators who still think that the system's formal channels of internal communication (e.g., meetings, memos, messages, directives, bulletins, notices, etc.) are the only meaningful sources of information within the organization. They're not wrong; they're just half right. (Unfortunately, no effective leader can afford to be only half right.)

Every organization, public or private, has a second communication system that is faster than a speeding bulletin and able to leap all barriers with a single bound. It's called the grapevine.

The grapevine is the informal, invisible internet that operates within every organization. It's not always accurate, but it's always fast and efficient. The typical grapevine is packed with information, misinformation, half-truths, untruths, gossip, guesswork, speculation, innuendos, and wishful thinking.

Rumors and gossip on the grapevine can take on lives of their own. The more they are repeated, the more credibility they assume.

Most grapevines are pervasive and persistent. No known administrator has ever successfully eliminated the rumor mill entirely from any group or organization.

Of course, not all rumors are bad. Some are innocuous. Occasionally, they can even serve a useful purpose, such as helping to create a group identity, providing a little excitement or entertainment within the organization, allowing people to blow off steam, or surfacing collective solutions to unspoken problems.

Nevertheless, grapevines also have awesome power for doing harm and have been known to crush careers and ruin lives. They are not to be taken lightly.

Some managers may ignore the grapevine or even join in it, but as chief communicator, no self-respecting leader can do either. Effective leaders respect the rumor mill, pay attention to it, and use it to their advantage, but they don't rely on it for valuable information or resort to using it to spread information themselves. (Once a leader is tainted by participating in gossip or rumor-mongering, he or she is never perceived in the same positive way again.)

The grapevine's greatest benefit for leaders is as a gauge for measuring the concerns and misconceptions that are bothering people at different levels of the organization. If people want to signal the leader that they're hurting or unhappy, they don't have to risk sharing the information directly. They can get their message across anonymously by using the grapevine.

Grapevines flourish most and are most troublesome in organizations that are unstable, where the trust level is low, and where communication is sparse. When staff and students feel left out, or that they're being kept in the dark, they try to read the handwriting on the wall or guess what's going on. That's when rumors start. That's also why full and open communication from credible leaders is the best defense against negative grapevine fallout.

As a leader, you will never be able to kill the grapevine completely, but you can manage it and keep it from doing undue damage to individuals, groups, or the organization as a whole. Following these commonsense steps is all it takes:

- Tell the truth—all of the time, not just some of the time.
- Be as open with bad news as you are with good news.
- Treat subordinates as adults capable of handling information responsibly.
- If you don't know, say so!
- Give everyone the same information.
- Pass on information in a timely manner before rumors can get up and running.
- Communicate face-to-face whenever possible.
- Never take action based solely on rumors or gossip.
- Don't comment on gossip or dignify it with a response except in emergencies.
- If a rumor is a lie, pounce on it and set the record straight as quickly as possible.

There are lots of legitimate ways for a leader to communicate within the organization. The grapevine isn't one of them. Savvy leaders establish themselves, rather than the grapevine, as the primary source of dependable insider information. It's not ego. It's their job.

If people trust the grapevine more than they trust you, you're not a real leader no matter what title you may hold. Being a leader means being believable. When people believe their leader, they're not as likely to trust the rumors or gossip that they pick up from the grapevine.

A NEW WRINKLE: THE ONE-MINUTE MANAGER MEETS THE TWO-MINUTE MIND

In addition to all the traditional challenges, there is a new communication concern that today's (and tomorrow's) school leaders cannot ignore.

It's no secret that life today is fast-paced, fragmented, and full of competing distractions. We live in a society saturated with sound bites and 60-second sermons. Increasingly, Americans expect (even demand) fast feedback, immediate answers, and instant gratification. As a result, we have a growing population with a shortened attention span. It's not just kids who can't sit still and pay attention very long any more. It's everyone.

Whether it's TV commercials, e-mail, voice mail, or text messaging, there isn't much in our society that requires sustained attention. Some observers say we now live in an era of the "two-minute mind."

Several years ago, legendary business guru Ken Blanchard coined the phrase, the "one-minute manager" to explain how supervisors can still have maximum impact even with limited direct, personal contact. Today, the one-minute manager has met the two-minute mind. (If you haven't noticed, you're not paying attention.)

Consequently, school leaders need to reexamine and adjust how they communicate with highly impatient and distractible audiences, including students, staff, parents, and the community at large. What many veteran administrators have found works best with inattentive listeners and readers is simply to

- Never assume that everybody "gets it" the first time. No matter what you say or how you say it, someone isn't listening or paying attention.
- Use multisensory communications (e.g., print, audio, and visual) as much as possible.
- Simplify the message.
- Shorten written communications. (The old business adage is truer than ever: "If it's stapled, it won't be read.")
- Use plenty of visuals. We live in a visual culture. The school is no exception.
- Do as much one-on-one communication as possible.

Of course, these strategies are what the best communicators have been doing all along.

Strangely enough, the 21st century's proliferation of communication technologies has not made communication much easier. Instead, it has created a crisis of information overload.

Effective school leaders today have to work harder than ever to get and hold the attention of diverse audiences and to make sure that their message gets through and gets heard.

25 WAYS SCHOOL LEADERS CAN IMPROVE COMMUNICATION

No school or business is any better than the quality of its internal and external communication. Open communication is the nutrient that nourishes all healthy organizations.

Guess what? It's the leader who always has primary responsibility for maintaining and improving this communication. If leaders do nothing more than open up the organization's communications inside and out, they've earned their keep. If you don't like communicating with all kinds of people, go to hermit school and forget about becoming an effective leader.

Anything you do to improve communication strengthens the organization and makes you a stronger leader at the same time. Following are 25 specific ways that you can communicate better with students, staff, parents, and the community at large, starting now:

1. Start a "Parenting Library" resource room or toy checkout center in the school.

2. Include an "open mike" segment at all PTA and PTSA or school board meetings.

3. Institute a hotline to provide community members with up-to-date school information.

4. Place school messages on billboards and marquees throughout the community.

5. Hold neighborhood and town meetings on important school issues.

6. Expand the number of advisory councils. How about an advisory council for athletics? Counseling services? School safety?

7. Provide incentives for teachers to make home visits.

8. Hold periodic evening and Saturday office hours.

9. Conduct concerts and other performances in the neighborhoods (in parks, parking lots, etc.).

10. Develop special "Parent Kits" with information on homework hints, summer activities, new opportunities for kids, and so on.

11. Place school newspapers and yearbooks in local physicians' and dentists' waiting rooms.

12. Develop an "Adult-in-the-School" program so that parents and other grown-ups can audit high school classes at no cost.

13. Conduct classes in local malls periodically so that shoppers can see students and teachers at work.

14. Convert an old school bus into a "School Mobile" to carry school displays throughout the community.

15. Encourage adult booster clubs for activities other than athletics, such as theater, debate, or band.

16. Organize a speaker's bureau of key staff members and students to make presentations to service clubs and other community groups.

17. Dare to be available to appear on local radio and TV call-in talk shows.

18. Develop an active alumni association and/or a historical society for your school.

19. Make it a point to set aside time each week to call parents of students who have extended illnesses and parents who normally are not involved in the school.

20. Develop special brochures for specific subgroups, such as 12th graders (graduating seniors), student athletes, business owners, and senior citizens.

21. Hold an activity fair to help students and parents learn about extracurricular activities. Include a "Name Your Activity" booth to solicit suggestions for new activities.

22. Conduct exit interviews with students and staff members who are leaving the school. Ask about what's working and what's not.

23. Ride the school bus a few times each year and listen to what students are talking about.

24. Check regularly with secretaries, custodians, counselors, and attendance clerks to find out what kinds of complaints they frequently receive.

25. Be sure that every school has a Web site on the Internet.

The strategies above can work anywhere. They also can serve as starter suggestions to help trigger more and better ideas. If you have what it takes to be a leader, you'll be able to think of many more. When you do, put them into action.

The point is to keep communicating. Communicate when there's good news. Communicate when there's bad news. Even communicate when there's no news. When you stop communicating, you stop leading.

If you want to lead, become the best communicator you can be. Good ideas and worthwhile plans often fail because they are not put across clearly and effectively. That's the leader's fault. Don't let it happen to you.

12

Practicing Ethical Leadership

This may be the most important chapter in this entire book, because without ethics, there is no point to leadership. Without a moral or values base, leadership is just personal aggrandizement in action, which is not a worthwhile subject for a book.

In a perfect society, the phrase "ethical leadership" would be a redundancy. In our culture, however, where scandals and allegations of misconduct involving political leaders and others in power positions pop up almost daily, leadership and ethics don't always seem synonymous.

There are many definitions of ethical behavior. One of the best is simply "doing the right thing at the right time for the right reasons." The problem is that the choices between right and wrong are not always clear today, and issues are not always black and white. We live in a world with a lot of gray in it. That's why many leaders-in-waiting are beginning to wonder if ethics are relevant any longer.

DO ETHICS MATTER ANYMORE?

Behaving ethically isn't always the norm anymore. We live in a somewhat jaded age in which self-preservation often prevails and everything seems to be negotiable—even moral values.

Daily headlines spotlight examples of unethical, dishonest, and immoral behavior on the part of politicians, entertainers, professional athletes, military personnel, government officials, and business leaders. Athletes shaving points, politicians taking bribes, trusted military leaders lying to Congress, and respected stockbrokers cheating on Wall Street have become commonplace. Where are the values in which our society is supposed to believe? Where are the leaders who live by them? Fortunately, many of them can still be found heading up the nation's schools.

Those who believe that you can't be completely ethical if you want to succeed today are wrong. The obvious isn't always the only reality. It may not be easy for some leaders to be ethical in contemporary society, but it is possible, and it is always worthwhile.

Some business officials may experience short-term success by using cutthroat, unethical methods, but moral misbehavior doesn't wear well in the marketplace for long. It doesn't wear at all in schools. Effective school leaders live their values just as they have always done. That's what the best principals and superintendents you know are doing every day.

In the long run, the most successful organizations are also the most moral. It's true in business, and it's especially true in the field of education. The best organizations, both public and private, continue to adhere to time-tested societal values and expect their leaders to do the same.

Good school leaders don't conduct business in a vacuum. They make decisions based on ethical values because they believe in them, because ethics are an integral part of the culture, and because it's expected. Ethics still count with kids, parents, and school boards.

Establishing a reputation for high ethical standards is one way a leader can build a better school. It helps attract the best people, helps them become peak performers because they feel good about where they work, and even helps them withstand crises. When things go wrong, doing right is always the best solution.

Ethical leadership sets a tone where values are contagious. It sends a powerful message about what's important, how people are to be treated, and how the school operates on a daily basis. It also requires that decisions be based on moral, as well as bottom-line, values. That's why today's successful principals and superintendents still hold strong beliefs and act on them every day. Ethical integrity and moral courage remain the trademarks of effective school leaders.

When moral dilemmas or choices occur, some administrators might equivocate, but true leaders always opt for the ethical response. So, do ethics matter anymore? You bet they do! Especially in schools.

WHY ETHICAL LEADERSHIP IN SCHOOLS IS DIFFERENT

School leaders are held to a higher standard. Period. Their ethical and moral behavior is judged against stricter criteria than is the behavior of leaders in many other fields. If you don't believe it, just ask any successful principal or superintendent.

The mayor, the governor, or even the president might be able to get away with improper conduct, like lying to the public or engaging in questionable financial dealings, but a local school official can't. The public has almost zero tolerance for misdoings by school personnel.

Holding a double standard for school officials may seem old-fashioned, but expecting exemplary behavior from those entrusted with the public's money and the public's children never really goes out of style. Likewise, expecting more from school leaders may not be fair, but it's the real world, and it's the only one in which we can live. You don't have to like it. You just have to accept it.

This stricter standard for school officials is too high for some wannabe leaders to accept. They don't want the scrutiny. They don't want the pressure. They don't really want to be true leaders if that's what it takes. They just want the authority (power), prestige, title, salary, and perks without the responsibility of such a heavy moral burden. They're out of luck. They can't have it both ways.

Leadership in any field carries high behavioral expectations. School leadership entails just a little extra emphasis on ethical conduct. Don't expect to become a full-fledged, effective school leader at any level unless you are willing to take on the full responsibility—including practicing principled behavior in and out of school, all day and every day. It may not be true in all fields, but in the education business, decency still works. Deceit doesn't.

For those who need convincing, there are some good reasons why school leaders face higher and harsher expectations than others do. Here are four worth noting:

1. *School leaders live in a bigger fishbowl.* They are the most public of public officials. They are more visible than most business or other leaders. They are not insulated by any artificial barriers. The doors of the neighborhood school are open to everyone every day.

School leaders are known throughout the community. Even the media know who they are. They're close, available, and accessible day and night. People are always watching. There's no place to hide. Consequently, squeaky clean behavior becomes their only viable option.

2. *Principled people expect principled leaders.* An unusually high level of ethical performance is a result of the self-fulfilling prophecy of the profession. The teaching profession tends to attract many idealistic men and women who champion family values and espouse old-fashioned virtues such as truthfulness, honesty, fidelity, and loyalty. They become teachers because they care and want to make a difference by helping others and instilling these values in future generations.

Many teachers will look up only to leaders who share their values and who demonstrate these characteristics in their daily living. Teachers and other school personnel may work for an unprincipled principal or superintendent; but they seldom work with one. They may show up, but they won't take the bait.

Because there are no leaders without followers, the best administrators just get used to living up to the higher expectations for ethical leadership. It's the price they pay for loyalty and support from those they lead.

3. *School leaders are still teachers.* People want their schools to exemplify the best that our society stands for. They still expect those who work in schools to be the role models that the rest of society doesn't always provide anymore.

It's important, then, that someone teach teachers, counselors, custodians, secretaries, aides, bus drivers, and others how to act. The leaders gets the call.

The principal and superintendent set the tone for the entire organization. By modeling ethical and principled conduct, they influence everyone else's behavior. A good sense of ethics by the leader instills respect and trust throughout the system. In all organizations, and especially in schools, people tend to live up (or down) to the image of the leader. Up is better.

4. *Children are involved.* The public not only entrusts school leaders with their tax money and expensive community facilities, they place in the school's keeping their most precious resource: their children and their children's future. Like it or not, this makes school leaders special in a way that doesn't apply to other forms of leadership.

Being a principal or superintendent may not be a sacred calling, but it comes close. Parents send the school their very best every day. That's why they expect a little more from their school leaders. They have a good argument.

Despite all this emphasis on exemplary behavior, school leaders don't have to be saints. Most school personnel still prefer to work for a regular human being.

Even the best leaders can and do make mistakes, suffer lapses in judgment, or fall prey to human frailty like everyone else. The good news is that in most cases, it is possible to recover from a temporary breach of ethics, regain trust and respect, and reclaim a valid leadership image. School leaders also get second chances like everyone else. The secret is prompt and honest admission, genuine remorse, scrupulous restitution, and a willingness to learn a hard lesson.

Of course, if an indiscretion or transgression is too serious, frequent, or consistent, any school leader can be quickly and unceremoniously defrocked. It makes headlines when it happens, because administrators can usually bounce back from minor infractions or violations of ethical conduct and continue on as strong and effective leaders. (Resiliency is an essential leadership trait.) Nevertheless, things may never be quite the same.

Even though mistakes have been corrected, amends have been made, and people have forgiven and forgotten, precious time has been lost and opportunities missed. What might have been may never be as once was possible. That's why the best advice is that if you can't follow the straight and narrow, let someone lead who can.

A single unethical act by a single unprincipled person can poison the entire organization. When that person is the leader, it can be a deadly dose.

Americans expect their school leaders to be unflinchingly caring, honest, truthful, ethical, moral, and upstanding. That's why school leadership is different. It's a lot to ask, but it's not too much. Isn't that the kind of leadership you want for your child's school?

THE CONCEPT OF "MORAL HAZARD"

In case there are any readers who don't believe 'or take seriously this discussion of ethics and school leaders, one more cautionary note is in order.

Social scientists and insurance company actuaries use the term "moral hazard" to describe a common phenomenon that is observable in a wide variety of entities, institutions, and organizations—including schools. Simply stated, the concept of moral hazard refers to the fact that when people know (or believe) they are shielded from some of the hazards associated with risky, amoral, immoral, or unethical behavior, they indulge in it more often.

The more people feel shielded from the natural consequences of their actions, the more likely they are to engage in misconduct. This isn't a universal tendency, but it happens often enough to be of concern. The concept of moral hazard applies to schools as much as to other organizations. It can topple school leaders as easily as it can other people.

Leadership is heady stuff. Principals and superintendents have power, authority, and freedoms that others don't have. They can get away with things that others can't. They have access to information, budgets, and resources that is denied to others. They know where the money is and how to get it.

Under these conditions, it can be easy to feel invulnerable and invincible. It may even be tempting to cut corners, cheat a little, or manipulate the system for personal gain. After all, who would know? Who would question? Who would challenge? Who would accuse?

The answer is that lots of people above, below, and all around a leader can bring down that leader for such misdoings. Teachers and other school personnel are not above whistle-blowing. Unions love to catch administrators off base so they can put them out. Irate parents are always looking for excuses to oust a leader they don't like. The media thrive on exposés. There's never a shortage of accusers when improprieties exist.

No matter how high up you climb or how powerful you become as a school leader, there is always someone higher or more powerful who can chew you out. No school leader is ever above the law, school board policy, or commonsense conventional ethics.

Some opportunistic administrators might be tempted by the concept of moral hazard. True leaders won't even think about it. That's why they're leaders. Anyone dumb enough to become a victim of moral hazard thinking is probably too dumb to be an effective school leader anyway.

USING VALUES AS A MORAL COMPASS: THIS IS NO TIME TO GET LOST

Q: What makes a courageous and passionate organization?

A: Shared values.

It's that simple. Without values, there is no vision. Without an unchanging core of basic beliefs, there is no meaningful leadership. Shared values give both the leader and the organization the courage and commitment to be proactive in pursuit of common goals.

The commonly held beliefs and moral commitments of the organization are the fixed points by which it charts its path and measures progress. They keep the system on course and moving in the right direction toward fulfilling its mission. Any time an organization sacrifices its values, it has thrown away its moral compass.

No school (or business) can know where to go or how to get there until it knows what it believes. Any organization that doesn't know what it values and stands for is lost in a sea of ambiguity from the very start. The leaders and followers alike are sunk before they ever get on board.

Shared values are what guide a successful school, or any other organization, toward better decisions. Ultimately, ethical leadership is mostly about making choices and doing the right thing based on a set of commonly accepted priorities. It's the leader's job to keep the organization true to these beliefs.

Some misguided administrators view beliefs and values as fluff—too nebulous to deal with. They're wrong. Actually, the opposite is true.

Values are the hard core of successful leadership in schools or anywhere else. Without a principle center, there is no solid foundation for visioning, planning, and decision making.

All of the best leaders in any field hold strong beliefs, act on them consistently, make decisions based on their values, and routinely function at a high level of moral courage and integrity. If you don't believe this, you'll probably always wonder why you didn't make it as a leader.

Don't be misled by the cynics on your staff who think that everything is relative and situational today, and that people can't agree on common values anymore. They're wrong. The old values are still there, and the time is always right for leaders to resurface, revisit, and restate them in order to better run their organizations.

Obviously, educators don't have a monopoly on values. More and more business leaders are showing an interest in basic beliefs and are initiating discussions about ethics within their organizations. Most business owners and CEOs still believe in certain time-honored values and want to embody them in the day-to-day operation of their companies. Good school leaders have always done this. If you haven't, it's never too late to get a good compass.

The critical link between values and leadership transcends all barriers and distinctions. It exists in all fields of human endeavor. Rob Lebow, a well-known business consultant, trainer, and author, has identified the following eight "people values" that are common to most organizations in both the public and private sectors:

1. Truth

2. Trust

3. Mentoring

4. Openness

5. Risk taking

6. Giving credit

7. Honesty

8. Caring

Similar findings resulted from a comprehensive 1998 study of visionary leaders in a variety of organizations, from museums to businesses to the Dutch colony of Aruba. The study was conducted by Visions and Values, one of the growing number of popular consulting firms dealing with shared values. According to founder Michelle Holt, "Visionary leaders share a sense of responsibility beyond their own life, a deep faith in people, a thirst for different perspectives, bravery and spirituality."

The lesson is clear: Principles, ethics, and moral values are prerequisites for effective leadership in all fields. If it's true for all visionary leaders, it must apply to your situation as well. Get the message?

Schools share many of the same values as successful organizations in other fields. They also have some unique ones of their own.

One of the critical values held by every effective school and school leader in the nation today is an abiding belief that all children can learn. As stated by Teacher Hall of Famer Owen M. Henson

We who are educators have no choice but to believe that all children have the capacity to learn and that the variables of poverty, dysfunctional families, drugs, single parent homes and crime are not valid excuses for us to avoid our responsibilities.

This is the kind of value that drives successful school administrators and their schools. It reveals the proper decisions to make. It generates commitment and passion. It shows the way. It's one of the compass points that gives the school clear direction.

If you're going to become an effective school leader and do more than mere management functions, you're going to have to be an ethical leader first and foremost. (Some successful principals and superintendents even write their own personal value statements and codes of conduct.) You must be principle centered to keep yourself focused as a leader and to model the school's basic values for others.

What you learned about values from parents, teachers, ministers, mentors, and others was part of your leadership training. You learned a lot from what these significant influences told you, but you learned even more from how they lived. Now it's your turn!

PRINCIPLES FOR PRINCIPALS AND OTHER ADMINISTRATORS

What does all this discussion about ethics for school leaders really mean for daily living? Anyone can claim values, talk morals, and preach ethics. Every manager and administrator you know can say the right words. Most do. The difference that often separates true leaders from the rest of the field is that leaders actually live the words. They practice what they preach. They walk the talk.

Some principals and superintendents believe that as long as they satisfy the requirements for holding an administrator's license, they're practicing acceptable ethical behavior. Give them credit for a good start.

Most states have identified certain grounds for suspending or revoking an administrator's license, such as the following:

- Immoral character or conduct
- Failure to honor a written contract
- Willful neglect of duty
- Fraud or misrepresentation in obtaining a license

Obviously, avoiding these license violations is part of ethical conduct. But it's not enough. Just obeying the law isn't enough, either. (Illegal behavior and unethical behavior aren't always the same. Professional standards are often higher than legal standards.) Even following all of the written school board policies and rules isn't enough. (Ethical leaders live by values, not just rules.) Then what does constitute "enough"?

Ethical behavior for school leaders means practicing honesty, fairness, decency, and compassion in all dealings and activities. If this sounds like a tall order, it is. Society has raised the bar for school leaders. This kind of exemplary performance and behavior stands out. That's why it's easy to recognize a real leader when you see one.

If you want to learn which principles the best principals, superintendents, and other administrators live by so that you can meet the standard, it's not hard to find out. You can readily spot those leaders who adhere to rigid ethical standards and value-based decision making. Here's how they act and what they do every day in and out of school:

1. Obey all applicable law and rules (this is the easy part).

2. Tell the truth.

3. Keep promises.

4. Accept blame.

5. Practice self-discipline.

6. Respect trusts and confidences.

7. Avoid half-truths.

8. Reward merit.

9. Give second chances.

10. Avoid using power or position for unfair advantage or personal gain.

11. Remain impartial, avoiding any hint of favoritism.

12. Demonstrate loyalty.

13. Respect privacy.

14. Avoid stereotyping or discrimination.

15. Behave in socially responsible ways.

16. Maintain personal integrity.

17. Respect everyone's rights.

18. Avoid even the appearance of impropriety.

19. Respect the dignity of others. (Ethical leaders avoid demanding unconditional surrender or humiliation from opponents.)

20. Avoid making decisions just because they will benefit themselves or their family, or just to make themselves look good.

21. Conserve resources and protect the environment.

22. Protect health and safety.

23. Avoid petty politics.

24. Take into account extenuating circumstances.

25. Refuse to cut corners.

26. Give credit.

27. Avoid accepting gifts or bribes in return for favors.

28. Give back to the community.

29. Promote the greatest good for the greatest number.

30. Constantly strive to get better.

You won't find these duties in your contract or job description, but they're essential expectations for all leaders. It's a big list, but being a leader is a big job. Despite these high standards, practicing ethical and moral behavior isn't some radical, far-right, overly pious, religious zealotry. It's just what good administrators have been doing all the time.

If you practice these principles in your daily affairs, you're going to have a hard time avoiding being taken for an effective school leader.

Why It Pays to Give Back to the Community

There are lots of good reasons for leaders to volunteer and get involved in giving back to the community. Here are some of the best:

- It's the right thing to do. ("Service is the rent we pay for living."—Marian Wright Edelman).

- It's the right time. With cutbacks in funding for social service agencies, now is the perfect time to reinvent the terms *community* and *good neighbor*.

- You're the *right* person. Everyone can help out in the community, but people with leadership skills can often help the most.

- It expands your network of contacts. Volunteering puts you into contact with leaders in other fields throughout the community.

- It sharpens existing skills. When you apply existing skills in an unfamiliar setting or situation, you always learn something new about them and get fresh feedback from new sources.

- You learn new skills. Volunteering lets you try new things in a non-threatening environment. Nobody expects a volunteer to be perfect.

- It feels good. There's true joy in helping others. It's better than a paycheck.

If you become involved in your community, you'll become a better leader. Better yet, you'll become a better human being.

A CODE OF ETHICS FOR TODAY'S SCHOOL LEADERS

The more closely a profession has responsibility for other people's resources and the public well-being, the greater the need for a clearly defined code of ethics. Drug dealers probably don't have a great need for a code of ethics, but doctors, lawyers, and CPAs do. Most of all, educators do.

A code of ethics is more than just a list of lofty ideals. It's a "do's and don'ts" directory of the right ways to act. It's a practical guide to honoring the highest standards of professional performance. A code of ethics defines appropriate day-to-day ethical conduct and moral behavior. It's the way professionals do business. If you want to become an effective school leader, try living and working each day by the guidelines spelled out in the code of ethics for the profession.

Ethics are for everyone. That's why all the professional education organizations (i.e., the NEA, AFT, NAESP, NASSP, and AASA) have adopted a code of conduct for its members. Many states are now enacting even stricter codes of ethics for school administrators that carry stiff penalties for any violations. Some principals and superintendents draw up their own personal codes or adopt one for their school. You may want to also.

As a leader, the important point is to know what the professional code of ethics requires and to follow it all the time. The tenets of your profession's code of ethics aren't hypotheses to be debated, they're words to live by. They're not goals, they're givens.

Some educators think that formal codes are unnecessary because all responsible people know how to act. The problem is that not all people are responsible, and not all responsible people agree. A written code of ethics eliminates all of the "I didn't know" or "I forgot" excuses for misbehavior.

There is power in writing down the ethical expectations for all members of the profession. The code becomes a covenant binding all parties to the same conditions and standards of conduct.

A good code of conduct spells out all of the obligations that every administrator acquires upon entering the profession, including responsibilities to learners, staff, colleagues, the community, and the profession. To be workable, it must be widely applicable, legally defensible, and observably measurable. Naturally, it needs to be reviewed and updated periodically.

If you are unfamiliar with the code of ethics for your area or organization, or if you want to develop your own, see the below sample codes of ethics.

Written codes of ethics take the guesswork out of moral professional behavior. If you have questions about how to act as a professional leader, go to your code of ethics for the answer.

Ethics are an attitude, a habit, and a choice that all principled school leaders make. Before reaching a tough decision, they ask themselves (consciously or unconsciously), "Do I feel right about this?" or "Will I be proud of this later on?" That's why they sleep better and like what they see in the mirror more than do less conscientious administrators. The greater a leader's self-respect, the more ethical his or her decisions are likely to be.

Not everyone can be the smartest kid on the block. Not everyone can be handsome or beautiful. Not everyone can be glib. Not everyone can be charismatic. But everyone can be ethical. When it comes to leadership, that's what's most important!

An educational administrator's professional behavior must conform to an ethical code. The code must be idealistic and, at the same time, practical so that it can apply reasonably to all educational administrators. The administrator acknowledges that the schools belong to the public they serve for the purpose of providing educational opportunities for all. However, the administrator assumes responsibility for providing professional leadership in the school and community. The responsibility requires the administrator to maintain standards of exemplary professional conduct. It must be recognized that the administrator's actions will be viewed and appraised by the community, professional associates, and students. To these ends, the administrator subscribes to the following statements of standards.

Code of Ethics for Minnesota School Administrators (adopted by MASA Board of Directors)

The educational administrator:

- Makes the well-being of students the fundamental value of all decision making and actions
- Fulfills professional responsibilities with honesty and integrity
- Supports the principle of due process and protects the civil and human rights of all individuals
- Obeys local, state, and national laws and does not knowingly join or support organizations that advocate, directly or indirectly, the overthrow of the government
- Implements the governing board of education's policies and administrative rules and regulations
- Pursues appropriate measures to correct those laws, policies, and regulations that are not consistent with sound educational goals
- Avoids using positions for personal gain through political, social, religious, economic, or other influence
- Accepts academic degrees or professional certification only from duly accredited institutions
- Maintains the standards and seeks to improve the effectiveness of the profession through research and continuing professional development
- Honors all contracts until fulfillment, release, or dissolution is mutually agreed upon by all parties to the contract

Recommendation for a Code of Ethics
for Supervisory Personnel

The professional school administrator:

Protection/Discriminatory Acts

1. Shall make reasonable efforts to protect learners and staff from conditions harmful to health and safety.

2. Shall take reasonable actions in exercising authority to provide an atmosphere conducive to learning.

3. Shall not misuse professional relations with learners, parents/caregivers, staff, or colleagues to private advantage.

Confidential Information

4. Shall disclose confidential information about individuals only when a compelling professional purpose is served in accordance with state and federal laws and school district policies.

Misrepresentation or Falsification

5. Shall not knowingly falsify or misrepresent records or facts relating to one's own qualifications or the qualifications of other staff or personnel.

6. Shall not knowingly make false or malicious statements about learners, their families, staff, or colleagues.

7. Shall accept no gratuities, gifts, or favors that impair professional judgment nor offer any favor, service, or item of value to obtain special advantage.

Unauthorized Professional Practice

8. Shall accept a contract for a position only when properly licensed or otherwise authorized by the State Board of Education.

9. For positions that require licensure, shall employ, recommend for employment, and assign only people licensed, or people who have been lawfully authorized by the appropriate state board or agency.

10. Shall comply with all state and federal laws, rules of the State Board of Education, and district policies.

Public Funds and Property

11. Shall manage, authorize the use of, and account for public funds and property for the purposes for which they are legally intended.

12. Shall not engage in conduct involving dishonesty, fraud, or misrepresentation in the performance of professional duties.

13

A Final Word

This entire text is a definition of leadership. If you need something more succinct, however, it ultimately boils down to this: An effective school leader is someone who

- Cares more than most
- Puts vision into words and words into action
- Sees more good than bad
- Has enough hope to spare and share
- Behaves as a positive role model
- Accepts responsibility
- Makes decisions
- Solves problems
- Stays calm
- Gets others to work
- Gives constant encouragement
- Earns respect
- Is kind in the process

Good schools need good leaders more than ever. Bad schools need them even more. Yours may need one most of all.

It's OK if you're content to be a caretaker manager, maintain the status quo, run the daily affairs of the school, protect and preserve its traditions, and keep everything operating smoothly as it always has. That's important and worthwhile. But occasionally, every school needs a leader who does more—a leader who rekindles the passion, clarifies the vision, and breathes new life into the organization. You could be that leader.

No one picks the time to become a leader. It picks them. Opportunities come to those who are prepared to receive them. Are you ready?

You know in your heart of hearts when you're just getting by day to day as an administrator, but how do you know when you're doing it right?

YOU KNOW YOU'RE A LEADER WHEN. . . .

You will know that you're really functioning as an effective school leader when

- People aren't afraid to bring you bad news.
- Your office is always crowded with people who are there not just to complain but to pitch in.
- Respected leaders from other schools ask your advice.
- The organization runs as well (or better) when you're absent as when you're present.
- Your staff members start getting more recognition and awards than you do.
- You can finish reading this book and truthfully say, "I already know all that stuff!"

LEADERSHIP IS A CHOICE

Leadership isn't a title or an entitlement. It's not a right or a gift. It's your decision. You can become an effective school leader if you make up your mind to be one. This book can help.

You may not be a Washington or a Lincoln or a Churchill or a Kennedy, but you're enough, if you want to be. Don't spend your time pining or whining. Lead, follow, or get out of the way. It's your choice.

Resource A

105 WAYS TO BE A BETTER
SCHOOL LEADER TOMORROW

1. Analyze a past mistake.
2. Stick your neck out for something you believe is right.
3. Reach for something a little beyond your grasp.
4. Plan a least one way to streamline your work.
5. Share information.
6. Promote someone from within.
7. Write legibly.
8. Don't hide behind your telephone.
9. Get enough rest.
10. Use plain talk—all the time.
11. Put off procrastinating.
12. Be on time—every time.
13. Shut up. Listen more.
14. Go out of your way for someone else.
15. Help someone who needs it.
16. Let other adults call you by your first name.
17. Get your own coffee.
18. Work beyond your contract or job description.
19. Learn something new—about your students, your job, or yourself.
20. Clean up your own mess.

21. Stay home if you're sick.

22. Be a cheerleader for others.

23. Push for higher standards.

24. Treat visitors like guests.

25. Don't be embarrassed to volunteer.

26. Call students by name.

27. Get back to someone in record time.

28. Remember birthdays and other important things about the people you supervise.

29. Think of a better way to do something.

30. Be more upbeat.

31. Set aside time to think, plan, and dream.

32. Eliminate one unnecessary rule.

33. Give someone a second chance.

34. Be a teacher.

35. Be a friend to someone (student or adult) who needs one.

36. Visualize success. Hold that thought.

37. Ask for help where you need it.

38. Steal a good idea—and give credit to the originator.

39. Impose a quiet time (an electronic turn-off period—no computers, no e-mail, no voice mail, no faxes) so people can think, work, plan, and dream in peace.

40. Replace some of the power symbols (e.g., flags, pictures of political leaders) around the school with affective symbols (e.g., plants, artwork).

41. Forgo complaining about job stresses, pressures, problems, or conflicts for one day.

42. Stop oversupervising.

43. Work for quality, not quantity.

44. Read an article or start a book on leadership.

45. Limit the number of times one person can speak at staff meetings.

46. Resist the urge to pass the buck.

47. Get back in person to someone with a complaint.

48. Add a new contact to your network of professional peers and colleagues.

49. Give up some of your budget and transfer the funds to a department that needs it more.

50. Show someone how excited you are about learning.

51. Let someone blow off steam without getting mad or getting even.

52. Arrange for an escort for female employees to the parking area after dark.

53. Give a promising staff member an exciting new challenge or opportunity.

54. Learn how to do something new on the computer.

55. Smile more.

56. Eat lunch with some staff members you don't see very often. Better yet, eat lunch with some students you don't know.

57. Give yourself an "idea quota" (e.g., at least one new idea per month).

58. Hire one of your staff members as a consultant on an important project.

59. Memorize your school's mission statement.

60. Reevaluate the balance in your life. Make whatever changes are necessary to live your priorities.

61. Patch up a quarrel with a subordinate or colleague. Compromise or agree to disagree if necessary.

62. Do something in your job or personal life that really scares you. (It's a powerful way to grow.)

63. Get current with your looks and wardrobe.

64. Get your personal and financial affairs in order. (It will give you more energy.)

65. Do something to make your school a kinder, gentler environment in which people can work and learn.

66. Give yourself permission to take more risks.

67. Plan a new way to have fun with your staff. (How about surprising them with an after-school root beer float bar?)

68. Pay attention. Show your interest.

69. Cancel one meeting that everyone can live without.

70. Give up on a bad idea.

71. Quit covering for or enabling an incompetent colleague.

72. Don't waste any time or stuff.

73. Start remembering people's names. Pay attention when you're introduced.

74. Do something unpopular that you know is the right thing to do.

75. Find a new mentor or become one yourself.

76. Correct a bad personal habit.

77. Start writing down daily goals. (You'll be surprised what a difference it makes.)

78. Surprise someone by giving him or her credit.

79. Say no to something you don't want to do.

80. Refuse to make a decision or take action when you're angry.

81. Bite your tongue. Avoid sarcasm.

82. Bite the bullet—tell someone what they're doing wrong and offer to help them do it right.

83. Don't brag.

84. Don't nag.

85. Thank someone (or several someones).

86. Spend more time out of your office.

87. Let your secretary tell you what stinks about your memos.

88. Make an extra effort to get your staff the best and latest materials and supplies.

89. Encourage your assistants to take their vacation time.

90. Don't take work home.

91. Show appreciation to a vendor who deserves it.

92. Spend some time with your custodians.

93. Help a staff member work on a difficult problem or project.

94. Do something extra to help a beginner.

95. Send some parents some good news.

96. Poll your clerical staff on how to improve office ergonomics.

97. Walk away from gossip.

98. Resist saying "I told you so."

99. Admit it when you screw up.

100. Answer your own phone as much as you can.

101. Do something good for your body.

102. Hire a "career detective" to find out what others (including current and former bosses) are saying about you. It's a way to insure honest feedback.

103. Place a mirror by office telephones (especially the receptionist's phone), so staff members can see how they look when talking to callers. (A smile always shows up in the voice.)

104. Replace rectangular conference room and boardroom tables with round ones that blur status, allow face-to-face interaction, and facilitate communication.

105. Ask employees what motivates them and lead accordingly.

Resource B

WHAT OTHERS SAY ABOUT LEADERSHIP

- Leadership is action, not position.—Donald H. McCannon
- The only limits are, as always, those of vision.—James Broughton
- The boss drives his people; the leader coaches his.
  The boss uses authority; the leader wins goodwill.
  The boss keeps them guessing; the leader arouses their enthusiasm.
  The boss talks about "I"; the leader makes it "we."
  The boss makes work drudgery; the leader makes work a game.
  The boss says "go"; the leader says, "Let's go."—Ted Pollock

- Whether you think you can or think you can't—you are right.—Henry Ford
- Example is not the main thing in influencing others. It's the only thing.—Albert Schweitzer
- If you can't stand the heat, get out of the kitchen.—Harry S. Truman
- You're only as good as the people you hire.—Ray Kroc
- Reason and judgment are the qualities of a leader.—Tacitus
- The best executive is the one who has sense enough to pick good men to do what he wants done, and self-restraint enough to keep from meddling while they do it.—Theodore Roosevelt
- Not to decide is to decide.—Harry Coy
- Ability is the art of getting credit for all the home runs that somebody else hits.—Casey Stengel
- Persistence is your ace in the hole.—Michael Perry
- Pay attention. This is everything. Pay attention.—Bruce Taylor
- Bad news doesn't stop happening.—Unknown
- The will to win is not nearly as important as the will to prepare to win.—Unknown
- It's kind of fun to do the impossible.—Walt Disney
- The harder you fall, the higher you bounce.—Unknown
- A man, as a general rule, owes very little to what he is born with—a man is what he makes himself.—Alexander Graham Bell

- Things turn out best for people who make the best of the way things turn out.—John Wooden
- There's a better way to do it . . . find it.—Thomas Edison
- We are what we repeatedly do. Excellence, therefore, is not an act, but a habit.—Aristotle
- Eighty percent of success is showing up.—Woody Allen
- What keeps me going is goals.—Muhammad Ali
- Perpetual optimism is a force multiplier.—Colin Powell
- Hold yourself responsible for a higher standard than anybody else expects of you. Never excuse yourself.—Henry Ward Beecher
- Subordinates should be more than an audience.—Unknown
- Problems are only opportunities in work clothes.—Henry J. Kaiser
- Keep company with those who make you better.—English saying
- If I had eight hours to chop down a tree, I'd spend six sharpening my axe.—Abraham Lincoln
- Be a good listener. Your ears will never get you in trouble.—Frank Tyger
- I'm a great believer in luck, and I find the harder I work, the more I have of it.—Thomas Jefferson
- There is no future in any job. The future lies in the man who holds the job.—George Crane
- I will prepare and someday my chance will come.—Abraham Lincoln
- Failure to prepare is preparing to fail.—John Wooden
- It's not whether you get knocked down; it's whether you get up.—Vince Lombardi
- Always do more than is required of you.—George S. Patton
- One man of courage makes a majority.—Andrew Jackson
- Just when you see the light at the end of the tunnel, someone adds more tunnel.—Jim Benson
- Try to be newer every day.—Unknown
- You can't make an omelet without breaking eggs.—Proverb
- Ever tried? Ever failed? No matter. Try again. Fail again. Fail better.—Samuel Beckett
- Being powerful is like being a lady. If you have to tell people you are, you aren't.—Margaret Thatcher
- Most people would die sooner than think. Most do.—Bertrand Russell
- A leader is one who accomplishes the goals of the organization without sacrificing core values.—Dennis Perkins
- The only thing worse than being the boss is not being the boss.—Dale Dauten
- You can't lead where you won't go.—Bumper sticker
- A principal has to be a spiritual leader.—Lee G. Bolman
- Everything rises and falls on leadership.—John C. Maxwell

Resource C

A BEGINNING BIBLIOGRAPHY FOR SCHOOL LEADERS

Anderson, P. (1990). *Great quotes from great leaders.* Lombard, IL: Celebrating Excellence.

Barth, R. (2003). *Lessons learned: Shaping relationships and the culture of the workplace.* Thousand Oaks, CA: Corwin.

Blanchard, K. (1998). *Gung ho: Turning on the people in any organization.* New York: Morrow.

Blanchard, K., & Johnson, S. (1982). *One minute manager.* New York: Berkley.

Blase, J., & Blase, J. (2003). *Handbook of instructional leadership* (2nd ed.). Thousand Oaks, CA: Corwin.

Blaydes, John. (2004) *Survival skills for the principalship.* Thousand Oaks, CA: Corwin.

Covey, S. (1989). *The 7 habits of highly effective people.* New York: Simon & Schuster.

Daresh, J. D., & Playko, M. C. (2001). *Beginning the principalship* (2nd ed.). Thousand Oaks, CA: Corwin.

Edelman, M. W. (1992). *The measure of our success.* Boston: Beacon.

Fullan, M. (2004). *Leadership and sustainability: Strategic thinkers in action.* Thousand Oaks, CA: Corwin.

George, B. (2003). *Authentic leadership.* San Francisco, CA: Jossey-Bass.

Hold, M. (1998). *Dreammakers: Putting vision and values to work.* Palo Alto, CA: Davies-Black.

Hoyle, J. P. (2003). *Leadership and the force of love: Six keys to motivating with love.* Thousand Oaks, CA: Corwin.

Lebow, R. (1998). *Lasting change: The shared values process that makes companies great.* New York: Van Nostrand Reinhold.

Machiavelli, N. (1997). *The prince* (A.M. Corevilla, Trans.). New Haven, CT: Yale University Press.

Morem, S. (1997). *How to gain a professional edge.* Fairfield, IA: Better Books.

Pellicer, L. (2003). *Caring enough to lead: How reflective thought leads to moral leadership* (2nd ed.). Thousand Oaks, CA: Corwin.

Pitino, R. (1997). *Success is a choice.* New York: Bantam.

Ramsey, R. D. (1992). *Secondary principal's survival guide.* Englewood Cliffs, NJ: Prentice Hall.

Ramsey, R. D. (1996). *The principal's book of lists.* Englewood Cliffs, NJ: Prentice Hall.

Ramsey, R. D. (2003). *School leadership from A to Z.* Thousand Oaks, CA: Corwin.

Ramsey, R. D. (2005). *What matters most to school leaders.* Thousand Oaks, CA: Corwin.

Sennett, F. (2004). *400 quotable quotes from the world's leading educators.* Thousand Oaks, CA: Corwin.

Sigford, J. L. (2005). *Who said administration would be fun?* (2nd ed.). Thousand Oaks, CA: Corwin.

Willower, D. J., & Licata, J. W. (1997). *Values and valuation in educational administration.* Thousand Oaks, CA: Corwin.

Index

**CORWIN
PRESS**

The Corwin Press logo—a raven striding across an open book—represents the union of courage and learning. Corwin Press is committed to improving education for all learners by publishing books and other professional development resources for those serving the field of PreK–12 education. By providing practical, hands-on materials, Corwin Press continues to carry out the promise of its motto: **"Helping Educators Do Their Work Better."**